WHOSE LIFE IS IT ANYWAY?

BRIAN CLARK

Introduction and notes by
Ray Speakman

Heinemann Educational Publishers
Halley Court, Jordan Hill, Oxford OX2 8EJ
Part of Harcourt Education

Heinemann is the registered trademark of Harcourt Educational Limited

First published in 1978 by Amber Lane Press Ltd
First published in the *Hereford Plays* series by Heinemann Educational 1989
First published in the *Heinemann Plays* series 1993

18

A catalogue record for this book is available from the British Library on request.

ISBN 0 435 23287 8

Cover photo: Alamy
Typeset by TechType, Abingdon, Oxon
Printed in the UK by Clays Ltd, St Ives plc

CONTENTS

PREFACE

In this edition of *Whose Life is it Anyway?*, you will find notes, questions and activities to help in studying the play in class, particularly at GCSE level.

The introduction provides background information on the play's first production and the impact of subsequent adaptations, outlines some of the main issues explored and considers the central theme.

The activities at the end of the book range from straightforward *Keeping Track* questions which can be tackled at the end of each act to focus close attention on what is happening in the play, to more detailed work and essay questions on characters and themes in *Explorations*.

If you are already using the Hereford edition of *Whose Life is it Anyway?*, you will find that the page numbering in the actual playscript is the same, allowing the two editions to be used easily side by side.

INTRODUCTION

Whose Life is it Anyway? was originally written as a television play and first appeared in 1972. Later, in 1978, it became a hugely successful stage play – at the Mermaid Theatre with Tom Conti as Ken Harrison. The play's impact was so great that it was filmed in the United States with an American setting.

The play centres around Ken Harrison's determination to exercise a choice over his own life or death. Opposing him are the forces of medical bureaucracy. It is an unsentimental play in which the main character responds to his plight with wit and clarity, and argues his right to choose with power and persuasion. The case against him is put by various members of the medical profession with a good deal of humanity, so much so that the issues are presented in all their complexity. It is for this reason, in particular, that Brian Clark's play will make stimulating and provocative reading.

The *Questions and Explorations* which follow the text fall into three sections. *Keeping Track* contains questions to be looked at alongside a first reading. They are intended to help the reader to keep close track of the play and its arguments as they unfold, and to point towards the central issues in the action. You may organise these (and add to them) in any way you think appropriate to the group reading the play. They might form the basis of a reading 'journal' or be grouped together to make a coursework assignment. *Explorations* presents a series of extension ideas which invite a creative response to the issues and situations in the play and which might act as a starting point for quite extensive pieces of coursework. Finally, there are some critical *Essay questions*. As well as turning the student back into the text to look at it closely, the activities provide the basis of a wider consideration of individual choice and free will.

Like all good plays, *Whose Life is it Anyway?* presents complex situations and arguments which will promote discussion and disagreement. The text will bear close examination and lengthy consideration. Furthermore, Brian Clark poses one of the 'big' questions about life – one which goes beyond the bounds of the particular situation it describes: do I have free will – who knows what is best for me – am I the best person to choose what I can and cannot do?

Ray Speakman

Details of First TV and Stage Productions

The first television performance of *Whose Life is it Anyway?* was transmitted on 12th March 1972 by Granada TV. It was produced by Peter Eckersley and directed by Richard Everitt, with Ian McShane as Ken, Susanne Neve as Dr Scott and Philip Latham as Dr Emerson.

The first stage performance was given at the Mermaid Theatre, London, in association with Ray Cooney Limited on 6th March 1978. It was directed by Michael Lindsay-Hogg and designed by Alan Tagg, with the following cast:

KEN HARRISON	Tom Conti
SISTER ANDERSON	Jennie Goossens
KAY SADLER	Phoebe Nicholls
JOHN	Trevor Thomas
DR SCOTT	Jane Asher
DR EMERSON	Richard Leech
MRS BOYLE	Rona Anderson
PHILIP HILL	Richard Ireson
DR PAUL TRAVERS	Edward Lyon
PETER KERSHAW	Alan Brown
DR BARR	Peter Honri
ANDREW EDEN	Robert Gary
MR JUSTICE MILLHOUSE	Sebastian Shaw

Characters in Order of Appearance

KEN HARRISON	The Patient
SISTER ANDERSON	Ward Sister
KAY SADLER	A Probationer Nurse
JOHN	A West Indian Ward Orderly
DR CLARE SCOTT	Junior Registrar
DR MICHAEL EMERSON	Consultant Physician
MRS GILLIAN BOYLE	A Medical Social Worker
PHILIP HILL	Ken's Solicitor
DR PAUL TRAVERS	Consultant Psychiatrist
PETER KERSHAW	Ken's Barrister
DR BARR	Consultant Psychiatrist (from Norwood Park Hospital)
ANDREW EDEN	Hospital's Barrister
MR JUSTICE MILLHOUSE	Judge

The action is continuous and takes place in a side ward, offices, corridors and a road outside a general hospital.

ACT ONE

SISTER ANDERSON *and* NURSE KAY SADLER *enter with trolley.*

SISTER Good morning Mr Harrison. A new face for you today.

KEN That's nice.

NURSE Hello.

KEN Hello, I'm afraid I can't offer you my hand. You'll just have to make do with my backside like all the other nurses.

They lower the bed.

KEN Going down – Obstetrics, Gynaecology, Lingerie, Rubber wear.

They roll KEN *over and start to massage his back with spirit and talc.*

KEN It's funny you know. I used to dream of situations like this.

SISTER Being injured?

KEN No! Lying on a bed being massaged by two beautiful women.

SISTER (*mock serious*): If you go on like this Mr Harrison I shan't be able to send my young nurses in here.

KEN They're perfectly safe with me, Sister.

The phone rings outside.

SISTER Can you manage for a moment Nurse?

NURSE Oh, yes Sister.

SISTER Wipe your hands and put the pillows behind Mr Harrison; we don't want to have him on the floor.

KEN Have me on the floor Sister please. Have me on the floor.

SISTER *goes out.*

KEN What's your name?

NURSE Kay.

KEN That's nice, but don't let Sister hear you say that.

NURSE What?

KEN What's your second name?

NURSE Sadler.

KEN Then you must answer 'Nurse Sadler' with a smile that is full of warmth, but with no hint of sex.

NURSE I'm sorry.

KEN I'm not. I'm glad you're called Kay. I shall call you Kay when we're alone, just you and me, having my back caressed . . .

NURSE I'm rubbing your heels.

KEN Well don't spoil it. After all it doesn't matter. I can't feel anything wherever you are. Is this your first ward?

NURSE Yes. I'm still at P.T.S.

KEN What's that? Primary Training School?

NURSE Yes. I finish next week.

KEN And you can't wait to get here full time.

NURSE I'll be glad to finish the school.

KEN All students are the same.

NURSE Were you a teacher?

KEN Tut tut; second lesson. You mustn't use the past tense.

NURSE What do you mean?

KEN You said: 'Were you a teacher?' You should have said: 'Are you a teacher?' I mean, you are now part of the optimism industry. Everyone who deals with me acts as though, for the first time in the history of medical science, a ruptured spinal column will heal itself – it's just a bit of a bore waiting for it to happen.

NURSE I'm sorry.

KEN   Don't be. Kay, you're a breath of fresh air.

SISTER *comes back.*

SISTER   Finished Nurse?

KEN   What do you mean? Have I finished Nurse. I haven't started her yet!

NURSE   Yes Sister.

They roll him back and remake the bed.

KEN   I must congratulate you Sister on your new recruit. A credit to the monstrous regiment.

SISTER   I'm glad you got on.

KEN   Well, I didn't get quite that far. Not that I didn't try Sister. But all I could get out of her was that her name was . . . Nurse Sadler . . . and that she's looking forward to coming here.

SISTER   If she still feels like that after being five minutes with you, we'll make a nurse of her yet.

KEN   I don't know quite how to take that, Sister – lying down I suppose.

SISTER   Night Sister said you slept well.

KEN   Ah, then. I fooled her . . . After her last round, a mate of mine came in and smuggled me out . . . We went midnight skateboarding.

SISTER   Oh yes . . . I hope it was fun . . .

KEN   It was alright . . . The only problem was that I was the skateboard.

SISTER   There, that's better. Comfortable?

KEN   Sister, it's so beautifully made, I can't feel a thing.

SISTER   Cheerio Mr Harrison.

They leave.

NURSE	Won't he ever get better, Sister?
SISTER	No.
NURSE	What will happen to him?
SISTER	When we have him fully stabilised, he'll be transferred to a long-stay hospital.
NURSE	For the rest of his life?
SISTER	Yes.

JOHN, *an orderly, comes along the corridor carrying shaving tackle on a tray.*

JOHN	Morning Sister.
SISTER	Morning John. Are you going to see Mr Harrison?
JOHN	That's right.
SISTER	He's all ready.
JOHN	Right.

JOHN *goes into the sluice room to collect an electric razor.*

NURSE	How long has he been here?
SISTER	Four months.
NURSE	How much longer will he be here?
SISTER	Not much longer now I should think. Take the trolley into the ward, Nurse. I should start on Mr Phillips.

SISTER *goes into her office.* JOHN *goes into* KEN'S *room. He plugs in the razor and shaves* KEN.

JOHN	Good morning Mr Harrison . . .
KEN	Come to trim the lawn?
JOHN	That's right.
KEN	Good . . . Must make sure that all the beds and borders are neat and tidy.
JOHN	That's my job.

KEN   Well, my gardening friend, isn't it about time you got some fertiliser to sprinkle on me and get some movement going in this plant?

JOHN   Ah, now there you have me. You see I'm only a labourer in this here vineyard. Fertilisers and pruning and bedding out is up to the head gardener.

KEN   Still, you must be in charge of the compost heap. That's where I should be.

SISTER *puts her head around the door.*

SISTER   John.

JOHN   Yes?

SISTER   Don't be long, will you. Dr Scott will probably be early today; there's a consultant's round this morning.

JOHN   Right Sister.

SISTER *goes back to her office.*

KEN   The visitation of the Gods.

JOHN   Eh?

KEN   The Gods are walking on earth again.

JOHN   Oh yes – they think they're a bit of alright.

KEN   What happened to the other chap – Terence he was called . . . I think?

JOHN   They come and they go . . . I think he left to get married up north somewhere.

KEN   Terence, getting married? Who to? A lorry driver?

JOHN   Catty!

KEN   No. Bloody jealous. From where I'm lying, if you can make it at all – even with your right hand – it would be heaven . . . I'm sorry . . . feeling sorry for myself this morning . . . can't even say I got out of the wrong side of the bed. Are you down to the bone yet? . . . Anyway, how long will you be staying?

JOHN Just till we go professional, man.

KEN Doing what?

JOHN Music. We got a steel band – with some comedy numbers and we're getting around a bit . . . We're auditioning for Opportunity Knocks in four months.

KEN That's great . . . Really great . . . I like steel bands . . . There's something fascinating about using oil drums – make something out of scrap . . . Why not try knocking a tune out of me?

JOHN Why not man!

He puts down his razor and, striking KEN *very lightly up and down his body like a xylophone, sings a typical steel band tune, moving rhythmically to the music.* KEN *is delighted.* DR SCOTT *comes in.* JOHN *stops.*

DR SCOTT Don't stop . . .

JOHN It's alright . . . I've nearly finished.

He makes one more pass with the razor.

KEN I was just making myself beautiful for you Doctor.

JOHN There . . . Finished.

He goes out the door.

KEN Work out some new tunes . . . Hey, if Doctor Scott could drill some holes in my head, you could blow in my ear and play me like an ocarina.

JOHN I'll see you later.

He grins and goes out.

DR SCOTT You're bright and chirpy this morning.

KEN (*ironically*): It's marvellous you know. The courage of the human spirit.

DR SCOTT (*dryly*): Nice to hear the human spirit's OK.

How's the lungs?

She takes the stethoscope from her pocket. She puts the stethoscope to KEN'S *chest.*

KEN   (*sings*): Boom boom.

DR SCOTT   Be quiet. You'll deafen me.

KEN   Sorry.

She continues to listen.

KEN   And what does it say?

DR SCOTT   (*gives up*): What does it say?

KEN   My heart, of course. What secrets does it tell?

DR SCOTT   It was just telling me that it's better off than it was six months ago.

KEN   It's a brave heart. It keeps its secrets.

DR SCOTT   And what are they?

KEN   Did you hear it going boom boom, like that? Two beats.

DR SCOTT   Of course.

KEN   Well, I'll tell you. That's because it's broken, broken in two. But each part carries on bravely yearning for a woman in a white coat.

DR SCOTT   And I thought it was the first and second heart sounds.

KEN   Ah! Is there a consultant's round this morning?

DR SCOTT   That's right.

KEN   I suppose he will sweep in here like Zeus from Olympus, with his attendant nymphs and swains.

DR SCOTT   I don't think that's fair.

KEN   Why not?

DR SCOTT   He cares; he cares a lot.

KEN   But what about?

DR SCOTT   His patients.

KEN I suppose so.

DR SCOTT He does. When you first came in he worked his guts out to keep you going; he cares.

KEN I was a bit flip, wasn't I . . .

DR SCOTT It's understandable.

KEN But soon we shall have to ask the question why.

DR SCOTT Why?

KEN Why bother. You remember the mountain laboured and brought forth not a man but a mouse. It was a big joke. On the mouse. If you're as insignificant as that, who needs a mountain for a mummy?

DR SCOTT I'll see you later . . . with Dr Emerson.

KEN And Cupbearers Limited.

DR SCOTT Oh no . . . I assure you . . . We're not all limited.

She goes out. She opens the door of SISTER'S *room. The* SISTER *is writing at the desk.*

DR SCOTT Sister. It's Mr Harrison. He seems a little agitated this morning.

SISTER Yes, he's beginning to realise what he's up against.

DR SCOTT I'm changing the prescription and putting him on a small dose of Valium. I'll have a word with Dr Emerson. Thank you Sister.

She closes the door and looks up the corridor towards KEN'S *room.* NURSE SADLER *is going in with a feeding cup.*

KEN An acolyte, bearing a cup.

NURSE I beg your pardon?

KEN Nothing. I was joking. It's nothing.

NURSE It's coffee.

KEN You're joking now.

NURSE   I'm not.

KEN   What you have there is a coffee-flavoured milk drink.

NURSE   Don't you like it?

KEN   It's alright, but I would like some real coffee, hot and black and bitter so that I could chew it.

NURSE   I'll ask the Sister.

KEN   I shouldn't.

NURSE   Why not?

KEN   Because in an hour's time, you'll be bringing round a little white pill that is designed to insert rose-coloured filters behind my eyes. It will calm me and soothe me and make me forget for a while that you have a lovely body.

NURSE   Mr Harrison . . . I'm . . .

KEN   (*genuinely concerned*): I'm sorry. Really, I *am* sorry. I don't want to take it out on you – it's not your fault. You're only a vestal virgin . . . Sorry I said virgin.

NURSE   You'd better drink your coffee before it gets cold. *She feeds him a little, sip by sip.*

KEN   I was right; it's milky . . . What made you become a nurse?

NURSE   I'm not a nurse yet.

KEN   Oh yes you are
        NURSE SADLER *smiles.*

KEN   *Nurse* Sadler.

NURSE   You must have thought me a real twit.

KEN   Of course not!

NURSE   The Sister-Tutor told us we could say it.

KEN   Well then . . .

NURSE   But I was so sure I wouldn't.

KEN   You haven't told me what made you become a nurse.

NURSE   I've always wanted to. What made you become a sculptor?

KEN   When you get a personal question, just ignore it –
change the subject or better still, ask another
question back.

NURSE SADLER *smiles.*

KEN   Did Sister-Tutor tell you to do that too?

NURSE   Something like it.

KEN   It's called being professional isn't it?

NURSE   I suppose so.

KEN   I don't want any more of that, it's horrid. Patients are
requested not to ask for credit for their intelligence,
as refusal often offends.

NURSE   You sound angry. I hope I . . .

KEN   Not with you Kay. Not at all. With myself I expect.
Don't say it. That's futile isn't it?

NURSE   Yes.

SISTER *opens the door.*

SISTER   Have you finished, Nurse? Dr Emerson is here.

NURSE   Yes, Sister. I'm just coming.

SISTER   Straighten the sheet.

NURSE SADLER *smooths the bed. She goes out as* DR
EMERSON *comes in with* SISTER *and* DR SCOTT.

DR EMERSON   Morning.

KEN   Good morning.

DR EMERSON   How are you this morning?

KEN   As you see, racing around all over the place.

DR EMERSON *picks up the chart and notes from the
bottom of the bed.*

DR EMERSON   (*to* DR SCOTT): You've prescribed Valium I see.

DR SCOTT	Yes.
DR EMERSON	His renal function looks much improved.
DR SCOTT	Yes, the blood urea is back to normal and the cultures are sterile.
DR EMERSON	Good . . . Good. Well, we had better go on keeping an eye on it, just in case.
DR SCOTT	Yes, of course sir.
DR EMERSON	Good . . . Well, Mr Harrison, we seem to be out of the wood now . . .
KEN	So when are you going to discharge me?
DR EMERSON	Difficult to say.
KEN	Really? Are you every going to discharge me?
DR EMERSON	Well, you'll certainly be leaving *us* soon, I should think.
KEN	Discharged or transferred?
DR EMERSON	This unit is for critical patients; when we have reached a position of stability, then you can be looked after in a much more comfortable, quiet hospital.
KEN	You mean you only grow the vegetables here – the vegetable store is somewhere else.
DR EMERSON	I don't think I understand you.
KEN	I think you do. Spell it out for me please. What chance have I of only being partly dependent on nursing?
DR EMERSON	It's impossible to say with any certainty what the prognosis of any case is.
KEN	I'm not asking for a guarantee on oath. I am simply asking for your professional opinion. Do you believe I will ever walk again?
DR EMERSON	No.
KEN	Or recover the use of my arms?
DR EMERSON	No.
KEN	Thank you.

DR EMERSON What for?

KEN Your honesty.

DR EMERSON Yes, well . . . I should try not to brood on it if I were you. It's surprising how we can come to accept things. Dr Scott has prescribed something which will help. (*to* DR SCOTT.) You might also get Mrs Boyle along . . .

DR SCOTT Yes, of course.

DR EMERSON You'll be surprised how many things you will be able to do. Good morning.

They go into the corridor area.

DR EMERSON What dose was it you prescribed?

DR SCOTT Two milligrams T.I.D.

DR EMERSON That's very small. You might have to increase it to five milligrams.

DR SCOTT Yes sir.

DR EMERSON We ought to aim to get him moved in a month at most. These beds are very precious.

DR SCOTT Yes.

DR EMERSON Well thank you Doctor. I must rush off. Damned committee meeting.

DR SCOTT I thought you hated those.

DR EMERSON I do, but there's a new heart monitoring unit I want . . . very much indeed.

DR SCOTT Good luck then.

DR EMERSON Thank you Clare.

He goes. DR SCOTT *looks in at* SISTER'S *office.*

DR SCOTT Did you get that Valium for Mr Harrison, Sister?

SISTER Yes Doctor. I was going to give him the first at twelve o'clock.

DR SCOTT Give him one now, will you?

SISTER Right.

DR SCOTT Thank you.

She begins to walk away, then turns.

DR SCOTT On second thoughts . . . give it to me. I'll take it. I want to talk with him.

SISTER Here it is.

She hands a small tray with a tablet and a feeding cup of water.

DR SCOTT Thank you.

She walks to KEN'S *room and goes in.*

DR SCOTT I've brought you something to help you.

KEN My God, they've got some highly qualified nurses here.

DR SCOTT Only the best in this hospital.

KEN You're spoiling me you know, Doctor. If this goes on I shall demand that my next enema is performed by no one less than the Matron.

DR SCOTT Well, it wouldn't be the first she'd done, or the thousandth either.

KEN She worked up through the ranks did she?

DR SCOTT They all do.

KEN Yes, in training school they probably learn that at the bottom of every bed pan lies a potential Matron. Just now, for one or two glorious minutes, I felt like a human being again.

DR SCOTT Good.

KEN And now you're going to spoil it.

DR SCOTT How?

KEN By tranquillizing yourself.

DR SCOTT Me?

KEN   Oh, I shall get the tablet, but it's you that needs the tranquillizing; I don't.

DR SCOTT   Dr Emerson and I thought . . .

KEN   You both watched me disturbed, worried even perhaps, and you can't do anything for me – nothing that really matters. I'm paralysed and you're impotent. This disturbs you because you're a sympathetic person and as someone dedicated to an active sympathy doing something – anything even – you find it hard to accept you're impotent. The only thing you can do is to stop me thinking about it – that is – stop me disturbing you. So I get the tablet and you get the tranquillity.

DR SCOTT   That's a tough diagnosis.

KEN   Is it so far from the truth?

DR SCOTT   There may be an element of truth in it, but it's not the whole story.

KEN   I don't suppose it is.

DR SCOTT   After all, there is no point in worrying unduly – you know the facts. It's no use banging your head against a wall.

KEN   If the only feeling I have is in my head and I want to feel, I might choose to bang it against a wall.

DR SCOTT   And if you damage your head?

KEN   You mean go bonkers?

DR SCOTT   Yes.

KEN   Then that would be the final catastrophe but I'm not bonkers – yet. My consciousness is the only thing I have and I must claim the right to use it, as far as possible, act on conclusions I may come to.

DR SCOTT   Of course.

KEN   Good. Then you eat that tablet if you want tranquillity, because I'm not going to.

DR SCOTT   It is prescribed.

KEN   Oh come off it Doctor. I know everyone around
here acts as though those little bits of paper have
just been handed down from Sinai. But the writing
on those tablets isn't in Hebrew . . .

DR SCOTT   . . . Well, you aren't due for it until twelve o'clock.
We'll see . . .

KEN   That's what I always say. If you don't know
whether to take a tranquillizer or not – sleep on it.
When you tell Dr Emerson, impress on him I don't
need it . . .

DR SCOTT smiles. She leaves and goes to the SISTER'S
room.

DR SCOTT   Sister, I haven't given it to him . . . Leave it for a
while.

SISTER   Did you alter the notes?

DR SCOTT   No . . . Not yet.

She picks up a pile of notes and begins writing.

(*Cross fade on sluice room.*)

NURSE SADLER *is taking kidney dishes and instruments
out of the steriliser.* JOHN *creeps up behind her and
seizes her round the waist.* NURSE SADLER *jumps, utters
a muffled scream and drops a dish.*

NURSE   Oh, it's you . . . Don't do that . . .

JOHN   I couldn't help myself, honest my Lord. There
was this vision in white and blue, then I saw red in
front of my eyes. It was like looking into a Union
Jack.

NURSE SADLER *has turned round to face* JOHN, *who has
his arms either side of her against the table.*

NURSE   Let go . . .

JOHN   What's a nice girl like you doing in a place like this?

NURSE   Sterilising the instruments . . .

JOHN *gasps and holds his groin.*

JOHN   Don't say things like that! Just the thought . . .

NURSE SADLER is *free and returns to her work.*

NURSE   I don't know what you're doing in a place like this .
. . It's just a big joke to you.

JOHN   'Course it is. You can't take a place like this seriously
. . .

NURSE   Why ever not?

JOHN   It's just the ante-room of the morgue.

NURSE   That's terrible! They don't all die.

JOHN   Don't they?

NURSE   No! Old Mr Trevellyan is going out tomorrow, for
instance.

JOHN   After his third heart attack! I hope they give him a
return ticket on the ambulance.

NURSE   Would you just let them die? People like Mr
Harrison?

JOHN   How much does it cost to keep him here? Hundreds
of pounds a week.

NURSE   That's not the point.

JOHN   In Africa children die of measles. It would cost only
a few pounds to keep them alive. There's something
crazy somewhere.

NURSE   That's wrong too – but it wouldn't help just letting
Mr Harrison die.

JOHN   No . . .

He goes up to her again.

JOHN   Nurse Sadler, when your eyes flash, you send shivers
up and down my spine . . .

NURSE John, stop it . . .

She is backing away.

JOHN Why don't we go out tonight?

NURSE I've got some work to do for my exam.

JOHN Let me help . . . I'm an expert on anatomy. We could go dancing, down to the Barbados Club, a few drinks and then back to my pad for an anatomy lesson.

NURSE Let me get on . . .

JOHN *holds* NURSE SADLER'S *head and slides his hands down.*

JOHN (*singing*): Oh the head bone's connected to the neck bone, The neck bone's connected to the shoulder bone, The shoulder bone's connected to the . . . breast bone . . .

NURSE SADLER *escapes just in time. She backs out of the room and into* SISTER, *who is coming to see what's causing the noise.*

NURSE Sorry Sister.

SISTER This hospital exists to cure accidents, not to cause them.

NURSE No . . . Yes . . . Sister.

SISTER Are you going to be all day with that steriliser?

NURSE No Sister.

She hurries away.

SISTER Haven't you any work to do, John?

JOHN Sister, my back is bowed down with the weight of all the work resting on it.

SISTER Then I suggest you shift some.

JOHN   Right.

She goes. JOHN *shrugs and goes.*

(*Cross fade on* DR EMERSON'S *office.*)

DR EMERSON *is on the 'phone.*

DR EMERSON   Look, Jenkins. I know the capital cost is high, but it would save on nursing costs. I've got four cardiac cases at the moment. With that unit I could save at least on one nurse a day. They could all be monitored in the Sister's room . . . Yes, I know . . .

DR SCOTT *knocks on the door. She goes in.*

DR EMERSON   Hello? . . . Yes, well old chap, I've got to go now. Do impress on the board how much money we'd save in the long run . . . alright . . . Thank you.

He puts the 'phone down.

DR SCOTT   Still wheeling and dealing for that monitoring unit?

DR EMERSON   Bloody administrators. In this job a degree in accountancy would be more valuable to me than my M.D. . . . Still, what can I do for you?

DR SCOTT   It's Harrison.

DR EMERSON   Some sort of relapse!

DR SCOTT   On the contrary.

DR EMERSON   Good.

DR SCOTT   He doesn't want to take Valium.

DR EMERSON   Doesn't want to take it? What do you mean?

DR SCOTT   He guessed it was some sort of tranquillizer and said he preferred to keep his consciousness clear.

DR EMERSON   That's the trouble with all this anti-drug propa-ganda; it's useful of course, but it does set up a negative reaction to even necessary drugs, in sensitive people.

DR SCOTT I'm not sure he's not right.

DR EMERSON Right? When you prescribed the drug, you thought he needed it.

DR SCOTT Yes.

DR EMERSON And when I saw him, I agreed with you.

DR SCOTT Yes.

DR EMERSON It's a very small dose – two milligrams T.I.D. wasn't it?

DR SCOTT That's right.

DR EMERSON The minimum that will have any effect at all. You remember I said you might have to go up to five milligrams. A psychiatric dose, you know, is ten or fifteen milligrams.

DR SCOTT I know, but Mr Harrison isn't a psychiatric case, is he?

DR EMERSON So how did you persuade him to take it?

DR SCOTT I didn't.

DR EMERSON Now let's get this clear. This morning when you examined him, you came to a careful and responsible decision that your patient needed a certain drug.

DR SCOTT Yes.

DR EMERSON I saw the patient and I agreed with your prescription.

DR SCOTT Yes.

DR EMERSON But in spite of two qualified opinions, you accept the decision of someone completely unqualified to take it.

DR SCOTT He may be unqualified, but he is the one affected.

DR EMERSON Ours was an objective, his a subjective decision.

DR SCOTT   But isn't this a case where a subjective decision may be more valid? After all, you're both working on the same subject – his body. Only he knows more about how he feels.

DR EMERSON   But he doesn't know about the drugs and their effects.

DR SCOTT   He can feel their effects.

DR EMERSON   Makes no difference. His knowledge isn't based on experience of a hundred such cases. He can't know enough to challenge our clinical decisions.

DR SCOTT   That's what he's doing and he's protesting about the dulling of his consciousness with Valium.

DR EMERSON   When he came in, shocked to hell, did he protest about the dextrose-saline? Or when he was gasping for breath, he didn't use some of it to protest about the aminophylline or the huge stat dose of cortisone . . .

DR SCOTT   Those were inevitable and emergency decisions.

DR EMERSON   And so is this one inevitable. Just because our patient is conscious, that does not absolve us from our complete responsibility. We have to maximise whatever powers he retains.

DR SCOTT   And how does a depressant drug improve his consciousness?

DR EMERSON   It will help him to use his consciousness Clare. We must help him now to turn his mind to the real problem he has. We must help him to an acceptance of his condition. Only then will his full consciousness be any use to him at all . . .

DR EMERSON   You say he refused to take the tablet?

DR SCOTT *nods.* DR EMERSON *picks up the 'phone and dials. The 'phone rings in the* SISTER'S *office.*

SISTER   Sister Anderson speaking.

DR EMERSON Emerson here. Could you prepare a syringe with five milligrams of Valium for Mr Harrison?

SISTER   Yes sir.

DR EMERSON I'll be down myself immediately to give it to him.

SISTER   Yes sir.

She replaces the 'phone and immediately prepares the syringe.

DR SCOTT   Do you want me to come?

DR EMERSON No . . . It won't be necessary.

DR SCOTT   Thank you.

She moves to the door.

DR EMERSON Harrison is an intelligent, sensitive and articulate man.

DR SCOTT   Yes.

DR EMERSON But don't undervalue yourself. Clare, your first decision was right.

DR SCOTT *nods and leaves the room. She is unhappy.*

DR EMERSON *walks to the* SISTER'S *room.*

DR EMERSON Have you the Valium ready Sister?

SISTER   Yes sir.

She hands him the kidney dish. DR EMERSON *takes it.*

SISTER *makes to follow him.*

DR EMERSON It's alright Sister. You've plenty of work I expect.

SISTER   There's always plenty of that.

DR EMERSON *goes into* KEN'S *room.*

KEN   Hello, hello, they've brought up the heavy brigade.

    DR EMERSON *pulls back the bed clothes and reaches for* KEN'S *arm.*

KEN   Dr Emerson, I am afraid I must insist that you do not stick that needle in me.

DR EMERSON   It is important that I do.

KEN   Who for?

DR EMERSON   You.

KEN   I'm the best judge of that.

DR EMERSON   I think not. You don't even know what's in this syringe.

KEN   I take it that the injection is one of a series of measures to keep me alive.

DR EMERSON   You could say that.

KEN   Then it is not important. I've decided not to stay alive.

DR EMERSON   But you can't decide that.

KEN   Why not?

DR EMERSON   You're very depressed.

KEN   Does that surprise you?

DR EMERSON   Of course not; it's perfectly natural. Your body received massive injuries; it takes time to come to any acceptance of the new situation. Now I shan't be a minute . . .

KEN   Don't stick that thing in me!

DR EMERSON   There . . . It's all over.

KEN   Doctor, I didn't give you permission to stick that needle in me. Why did you do it?

DR EMERSON   It was necessary. Now try to sleep . . . You will find that as you gain acceptance of the situation you will be able to find a new way of living.

KEN   Please let me make myself clear. I specifically refused permission to stick that needle in me and you didn't listen. You took no notice.

DR EMERSON   You must rely on us, old chap. Of course you're depressed. I'll send someone along to have a chat with you. Now I must go and get on with my rounds.

KEN   Doctor . . .

DR EMERSON   I'll send someone along.

He places the dish on the side locker, throwing the needle in a waste bin. He goes out. KEN *is frustrated and then his eyes close.*

(*Cross fade on* SISTER'S *office.*)

SISTER   I'm always warning my nurses not to get involved.

DR SCOTT   Of course . . . And you never do, do you?

SISTER   (*smiling*): . . . Never.

DR SCOTT   You're a liar Sister.

SISTER   Dr Scott!

DR SCOTT   Come on, we all do. Dr Emerson is as involved with Mr Harrison as if he were his father.

SISTER   But you don't feel like his mother!

DR SCOTT   . . . No comment Sister.

(NURSE SADLER *comes into* SISTER'S *office.*)

NURSE   I've finished Sister.

SISTER   Alright . . . Off you go then Nurse.

NURSE   Yes Sister!

SISTER   Have you been running?

NURSE   No Sister!

SISTER   Oh . . . You just looked . . . flushed.

NURSE   . . . Oh . . . Goodnight Sister . . . Doctor.

SISTER   Goodnight.

DR SCOTT   Goodnight.

(*Cross fade to* KEN'S *room.*)

SISTER *and* NURSE SADLER *come in with the trolley.*

SISTER Good morning Mr Harrison. How are you this morning?

KEN Marvellous.

SISTER Night Sister said you slept well.

KEN I did. I had a lot of help, remember.

SISTER Your eyes are bright this morning.

KEN I've been thinking.

SISTER You do too much of that.

KEN What other activity would you suggest? . . . Football? I tell you what Sister, just leave me alone with Nurse Sadler here. Let's see what the old Adam can do for me.

SISTER I'm a Sister not a Madame.

KEN Sister – you dark horse you! All this time you've been kidding me. I've been wondering for months how on earth a woman could become a State Registered Nurse and a Sister and still think you found babies under a gooseberry bush – and you've known all along.

SISTER Of course I've known. When I qualified as a midwife I learnt that when they pick up the babies from under the gooseberry bushes they wrap them up in women to keep them warm. I know because it was our job to unwrap them again.

KEN The miracle of modern science! Anyway, Sister, as I said, I've been thinking, if I'm going to be around for a long time, money will help.

SISTER It always does.

KEN Do you remember that solicitor chap representing my insurance company a few months ago? Mr Hill, I think he said his name was. Do you think you could get him back as soon as possible? I'd feel more settled if we could get the compensation sorted out.

SISTER	Sounds a good idea.
KEN	You'll ring him up?
SISTER	Of course.
KEN	He left a card; it's in my drawer.
SISTER	Right.

She goes to the locker and takes out the card.

SISTER Mr Philip Hill, Solicitor, Right, I'll ring him.

KEN Thanks.

SISTER That's enough.

They cover him up again and straighten the bed.

SISTER Mrs Boyle is waiting to see you Mr Harrison.

KEN Mrs Boyle? Who's she?

SISTER A very nice women.

KEN Oh God, must I see her?

SISTER Dr Emerson asked her to come along.

KEN Then I'd better see her. If I refuse, he'll probably dissolve her in water and inject her into me.

SISTER *has to choke back a giggle.*

SISTER Mr Harrison! Come on Nurse; this man will be the death of me.

KEN (*cheerfully*): Doubt it Sister. I'm not even able to be the death of myself.

SISTER *goes out with* NURSE SADLER, MRS GILLIAN BOYLE *enters. She is thirty-five, attractive, and very professional in her manner. She is a medical social worker.*

MRS BOYLE Good morning.

KEN Morning.

MRS BOYLE Mr Harrison?

KEN	(*cheerfully*): It used to be.
MRS BOYLE	My name is Mrs Boyle.
KEN	And you've come to cheer me up.
MRS BOYLE	I wouldn't put it like that.
KEN	How would you put it?
MRS BOYLE	I've come to see if I can help.
KEN	Good. You can.
MRS BOYLE	How?
KEN	Go and convince Dr Frankenstein that he has successfully made his monster and he can now let it go.
MRS BOYLE	Dr Emerson is a first-rate physician. My goodness, they have improved this room.
KEN	Have they?
MRS BOYLE	It used to be really dismal. All dark green and cream. It's surprising what pastel colours will do, isn't it. Really cheerful.
KEN	Yes; perhaps they should try painting me. I'd hate to be the thing that ruins the decor.
MRS BOYLE	What on earth makes you say that? You don't ruin anything.
KEN	I'm sorry. That was a bit . . . whining. Well don't let me stop you.
MRS BOYLE	Doing what?
KEN	What you came for I suppose. What do you do? Conjuring tricks? Funny stories? Or a belly dance? If I have any choice, I'd prefer the belly dance.
MRS BOYLE	I'm afraid I've left my bikini at home.
KEN	Who said anything about a bikini?
MRS BOYLE	Dr Emerson tells me that you don't want any more treatment.
KEN	Good.
MRS BOYLE	Why good?
KEN	I didn't think he'd heard what I'd said.

MRS BOYLE	Why not?
KEN	He didn't take any notice.
MRS BOYLE	Well as you can see, he did.
KEN	He sent you?
MRS BOYLE	Yes.
KEN	And you are my new treatment; get in.
MRS BOYLE	Why don't you want any more treatment?
KEN	I'd rather not go on living like this.
MRS BOYLE	Why not?
KEN	Isn't it obvious?
MRS BOYLE	Not to me. I've seen many patients like you.
KEN	And they all want to live?
MRS BOYLE	Usually.
KEN	Why?
MRS BOYLE	They find a new way of life.
KEN	How?
MRS BOYLE	You'll be surprised how many things you will be able to do with training and a little patience.
KEN	Such as?
MRS BOYLE	We can't be sure yet. But I should think that you will be able to operate reading machines and perhaps an adapted typewriter.
KEN	Reading and writing. What about arithmetic?
MRS BOYLE	(*smiling*): I dare say we could fit you up with a comptometer if you really wanted one.
KEN	Mrs Boyle, even educationalists have realised that the three r's do not make a full life.
MRS BOYLE	What did you do before the accident?
KEN	I taught in an art school. I was a sculptor.
MRS BOYLE	I see.
KEN	Difficult, isn't it? How about an electrically operated hammer and chisel? No, well. Or a cybernetic lump of clay?

MRS BOYLE   I wouldn't laugh if I were you. It's amazing what can be done. Our scientists are wonderful.

KEN   They are. But it's not good enough you see, Mrs Boyle. I really have absolutely no desire at all to be the object of scientific virtuosity. I have thought things over very carefully. I do have plenty of time for thinking and I have decided that I do not want to go on living with so much effort for so little result.

MRS BOYLE   Yes, well, we shall have to see about that.

KEN   What is there to see?

MRS BOYLE   We can't just stop treatment, just like that.

KEN   Why not?

MRS BOYLE   It's the job of the hospital to save life, not to lose it.

KEN   The hospital's done all it can, but it wasn't enough. It wasn't the hospital's fault the original injury was too big.

MRS BOYLE   We have to make the best of the situation.

KEN   No. 'We' don't have to do anything. I have to do what has to be done and that is to cash in the chips.

MRS BOYLE   It's not unusual, you know, for people injured as you have been to suffer with this depression for a considerable time before they begin to see that a life is possible.

KEN   How long?

MRS BOYLE   It varies.

KEN   Don't hedge.

MRS BOYLE   It could be a year or so.

KEN   And it could last for the rest of my life.

MRS BOYLE   That would be most unlikely.

KEN   I'm sorry, but I cannot settle for that.

MRS BOYLE   Try not to dwell on it. I'll see what I can do to get you started on some occupational therapy. Perhaps we could make a start on the reading machines.

KEN	Do you have many books for those machines?
MRS BOYLE	Quite a few.
KEN	Can I make a request for the first one?
MRS BOYLE	If you like.
KEN	'How to be a sculptor with no hands '.
MRS BOYLE	I'll be back tomorrow with the machine.
KEN	It's marvellous you know.
MRS BOYLE	What is?
KEN	All you people have the same technique. When I say something really awkward you just pretend I haven't said anything at all. You're all the bloody same . . . Well there's another outburst. That should be your cue to comment on the light-shade or the colour of the walls.
MRS BOYLE	I'm sorry if I have upset you.
KEN	Of course you have upset me. You and the doctors with your appalling so-called professionalism, which is nothing more than a series of verbal tricks to prevent you relating to your patients as human beings.
MRS BOYLE	You must understand; we have to remain relatively detached in order to help . . .
KEN	That's alright with me. Detach yourself. Tear yourself off on the dotted line that divides the woman from the social worker and post yourself off to another patient.
MRS BOYLE	You're very upset.
KEN	Christ Almighty, you're doing it again. Listen to yourself, woman. I say something offensive about you and you turn your professional cheek. If you were human, if you were treating me as a human, you'd tell me to bugger off. Can't you see that this is why I've decided that life isn't worth living? I am not human and I'm even more convinced of that by your visit than I was before, so how does that grab you? The very exercise of your so-called professionalism makes me want to die.

MRS BOYLE I'm . . . Please . . .

KEN Go . . . For God's sake get out . . . Go on . . . Get out . . . Get out . . .

She goes into SISTER'S *room.* SISTER *hears* KEN'S *shouts.*

SISTER What's the matter Mrs Boyle?

MRS BOYLE It's Mr Harrison . . . He seems very upset.

KEN (*shouting*): . . . I am upset.

SISTER *closes the door.*

SISTER I should leave him for now Mrs Boyle. We'll send for you again when he's better.

SISTER *hurries in to* KEN. *He is very distressed, rocking his head from side to side, desperately short of breath.*

KEN Sis . . . ter . . .

SISTER *reaches for the oxygen mask.*

SISTER Now, now, Mr Harrison, calm down.

She applies the mask and turns on the oxygen. KEN *gradually becomes calmer.*

SISTER Now why do you go getting yourself so upset? . . . There's no point . . .

KEN (*muffled*): But . . .

SISTER Stop talking Mr Harrison. Just relax.

KEN *becomes calm.* SISTER *sees* NURSE SADLER *going past.* MRS BOYLE *is still hovering.*

SISTER Nurse.

NURSE Sister?

SISTER Take over here will you?

NURSE   Yes Sister.

NURSE SADLER *holds the mask.* SISTER *goes to the door.*

MRS BOYLE   Is he alright?

SISTER   Yes, perfectly.

MRS BOYLE   I'm sorry . . .

SISTER   Don't worry. It was not you . . . We'll let you know when he's better.

MRS BOYLE   Right . . . Thank you.

She goes. SISTER *stands at the open door.*

SISTER   Just give him another ten seconds, Nurse.

NURSE   Yes Sister.

SISTER *takes a pace back behind the door and listens. After ten seconds,* NURSE SADLER *removes the mask.*

KEN   Oh, she's a shrewd cookie, is our Sister.

SISTER *smiles at this.* NURSE SADLER *glances backward.* KEN *catches on to the reason.*

KEN   It's alright Sister. I'm still alive, bugger it. I don't want to give her too much satisfaction.

NURSE   She's gone.

She closes the door.

KEN   Come on then, over here. I shan't bite you Kay. Come and cool my fevered brow or something.

NURSE   What upset you?

KEN   Being patronised did I suppose.

NURSE   What did you mean about Sister?

KEN   She knew if she came in I'd shout at her, but if you were here I wouldn't shout.

NURSE Why?

KEN A good question. Because I suppose you're young and gentle and innocent and Sister knows that I am not the sort who would shout at you . . .

NURSE You mean, you would rather patronise me.

KEN Hey! Steady on there Kay. If you show you're well able to take care of yourself I shall have to call you Nurse Sadler and shout at you too and Sister and I will have lost a valuable asset.

NURSE What were you . . . ?

The door opens and SISTER *and* DR SCOTT *come in.*

KEN What is this? Piccadilly Circus?

SISTER Alright Nurse. Dr Scott was just coming as it happened. Are you feeling better now Mr Harrison?

NURSE SADLER *leaves.*

KEN Lovely, thank you, Sister.

SISTER I made your 'phone call to Mr Hill. He said he'd try to get in tomorrow.

KEN Thank you . . .

SISTER *leaves.*

DR SCOTT And what was all the fuss about?

KEN I'm sorry about that. The last thing I want is to bring down Emerson again with his pharmaceutical truncheon.

DR SCOTT I'm . . . sorry about that.

KEN I don't suppose it was your fault.

DR SCOTT Can I give you some advice?

KEN Please do; I may even take it.

DR SCOTT Take the tablets; the dose is very small – the minimum – and it won't really blunt your consciousness, not like the injection.

KEN   . . . You're on.

DR SCOTT Good . . . I was glad to hear about your decision to try and get your compensation settled.

KEN   How did you know ? . . . Oh, I suppose Sister checked with you.

DR SCOTT She did mention it . . .

KEN   You have lovely breasts.

DR SCOTT I beg your pardon?

KEN   I said you have lovely breasts.

DR SCOTT What an odd thing to say.

KEN   Why? You're not only a doctor are you? You can't tell me that you regard them only as mammary glands.

DR SCOTT No.

KEN   You're quite safe.

DR SCOTT Of course.

KEN   I'm not about to jump out of bed and rape you or anything.

DR SCOTT I know.

KEN   Did it embarrass you?

DR SCOTT Surprised me.

KEN   And embarrassed you.

DR SCOTT I suppose so.

KEN   But why exactly? You are an attractive woman. I admit that it's unusual for a man to compliment a woman on her breasts when only one of them is in bed, only one of the people that is, not one of the breasts, but that wasn't the reason was it?

DR SCOTT I don't think it helps you to talk like this.   *

KEN   Because I can't do anything about it you mean.

DR SCOTT I didn't mean that exactly.

KEN   I watch you walking in the room, bending over me, tucking in your sweater. It's surprising how relaxed a woman can become when she is not in the presence of a man.

DR SCOTT I am sorry if I provoked you . . . I can assure you . . .

KEN You haven't 'provoked' me, as you put it, but you are a woman and even though I've only a piece of knotted string between my legs, I still have a man's mind. One change that I have noticed is that I now engage in sexual banter with young nurses, searching for the double entendre in the most innocent remark. Like a sexually desperate middle-aged man. Then they leave the room and I go cold with embarrassment. It's fascinating isn't it? Laughable. I still have tremendous sexual desire. Do you find that disgusting?

DR SCOTT No.

KEN Pathetic?

DR SCOTT Sad.

KEN I am serious you know . . . about deciding to die.

DR SCOTT You will get over that feeling.

KEN How do you know?

DR SCOTT From experience.

KEN That doesn't alter the validity of my decision now.

DR SCOTT But if we acted on your decision now, there wouldn't be an opportunity for you to accept it.

KEN I grant you, I may become lethargic and quiescent. Happy when a nurse comes to put in a new catheter, or give me an enema, or to turn me over. These could become the high spots of my day. I might even learn to do wonderful things, like turn the pages of a book with some miracle of modern science, or to type letters with flicking my eyelids. And you would look at me and say: 'Wasn't it worth waiting?' and I would say: 'Yes' and be proud of my achievements. Really proud. I grant you all

that, but it doesn't alter the validity of my present
position.

DR SCOTT   But if you become happy?

KEN   But I don't want to become happy by becoming the
computer section of a complex machine. And
morally, you must accept my decision.

DR SCOTT   Not according to my morals.

KEN   And why are yours better than mine? They're better
because you're more powerful. I am in your power.
To hell with a morality that is based on the
proposition that might is right.

DR SCOTT   I must go now. I was halfway through Mr Patel.

She walks to the door.

KEN   I thought you were just passing. Oh Doctor . . . one
more thing.

DR SCOTT   Yes?

KEN   You still have lovely breasts.

She smiles and goes out into the SISTER'S *office. She is
very upset.* SISTER *passes and looks at her.*

SISTER   Are you alright? Would you like a cup of tea?

DR SCOTT   Yes Sister, I would.

SISTER   . . . Nurse! Would you bring a cup of tea?

NURSE SADLER *looks from the kitchen.*

NURSE   Yes Sister.

They walk into the SISTER'S *room and sit down.*

DR SCOTT   I've never met anyone like Mr Harrison before.

SISTER   No.

DR SCOTT   He's so . . . bright . . . intelligent . . . He says he
wants to die.

SISTER   Many patients say that.

DR SCOTT   I know that Sister, but he means it. It's just a calm rational decision.

SISTER   I thought this morning, when he was talking about the compensation, he was beginning to plan for the future.

DR SCOTT   Not really you know. That was just to keep us happy. He probably thinks that if he pretends to be planning for the future we'll stop tranquillizing him or something like that.

A knock on the door.

SISTER   Come in.

NURSE   Here's the tea Sister.

SISTER   Thank you Nurse. For Doctor.

NURSE SADLER *gives the cup to* DR SCOTT *and goes out.*

DR SCOTT   It's marvellous you know. We bring him back to life using everything we've got. We give him back his consciousness, then he says: 'But how do I use it?' So what do we do? We put him back to sleep.

Cross fade on KEN'S *room.*

JOHN *goes in to empty the rubbish. He taps* KEN *lightly as if to repeat the steel band game but* KEN *is asleep.*

JOHN   Ping-pong . . . You poor bastard.

He leaves.

END OF ACT ONE.

ACT TWO

SISTER A visitor for you Mr Harrison.

HILL Good afternoon Mr Harrison.

KEN Good afternoon.

HILL You're looking very much better.

SISTER has placed a chair by the bed.

KEN It's the nursing you know.

SISTER I'm glad you realise it Mr Harrison.

KEN Oh I do Sister, I do.

SISTER I'll leave you gentlemen now.

HILL Thank you Sister.

She goes out.

HILL You really do look better.

KEN Yes. I'm as well now as I shall ever be . . .

HILL (*unzipping his briefcase*): I've brought all the papers . . . Things are moving along very satisfactorily now and . . .

KEN I don't want to talk about the accident.

HILL I understand it must be very distressing.

KEN No, no. It's not that. I didn't get you along about the compensation.

HILL Oh . . . Sister said on the 'phone . . .

KEN Yes, I know. Could you come away from the door? Look, do you work for yourself? I mean you don't work for an insurance company or something, do you? . . .

HILL No. I'm in practice as a solicitor, but I . . .

KEN Then there's no reason why you couldn't represent me generally . . . apart from this compensation thing . . .

HILL Certainly, if there's anything I can do . . .

KEN There is.

HILL Yes?

KEN . . . Get me out of here.

HILL . . . I don't understand, Mr Harrison.

KEN It's quite simple. I can't exist outside the hospital, so they've got to keep me here if they want to keep me alive and they seem intent on doing that. I've decided that I don't want to stay in hospital any longer.

HILL But surely they wouldn't keep you here longer than necessary?

KEN I'm almost completely paralysed and I always will be. I shall never be discharged by the hospital. I have coolly and calmly thought it out and I have decided that I would rather not go on. I therefore want to be discharged to die.

HILL And you want me to represent you?

KEN Yes. Tough.

HILL . . . And what is the hospital's attitude?

KEN They don't know about it yet. Even tougher.

HILL This is an enormous step . . .

KEN Mr Hill, with all respect, I know that our hospitals are wonderful. I know that many people have succeeded in making good lives with appalling handicaps. I'm happy for them and respect and admire them. But each man must make his own decision. And mine is to die quietly and with as much dignity as I can muster and I need your help.

HILL Do you realise what you're asking me to do?

KEN I realise. I'm not asking that you make any decision about my life and death, merely that you represent me and my views to the hospital.

HILL . . . Yes, well, the first thing is to see the Doctor. What is his name?

KEN Dr Emerson.

HILL   I'll try and see him now and come back to you.

KEN   Then you'll represent me?

HILL   Mr Harrison, I'll let you know my decision after I've seen Dr Emerson.

KEN   Alright, but you'll come back to tell me yourself, even if he convinces you he's right?

HILL   Yes, I'll come back.

Cross fade on the sluice room.

NURSE SADLER *and* JOHN *are talking.*

JOHN   So why not? . . .

NURSE   It's just that I'm so busy . . .

JOHN   All work and no play . . . makes for a boring day.

NURSE   Anyway, I hardly know you.

JOHN   Right . . . That's why I want to take you out . . . to find out what goes on behind those blue eyes . . .

NURSE   At present, there's just lists of bones and organs, all getting themselves jumbled up.

JOHN   Because you're working them too hard . . .

NURSE   Ask me next week . . .

JOHN   OK. It's a deal . . .

NURSE   Right!

JOHN   And I'll ask you this afternoon as well.

Cross fade on DR EMERSON'S *room.*

DR EMERSON   Mr Hill? Sister just rang through.

HILL   Dr Emerson?

They shake hands.

DR EMERSON   You've been seeing Mr Harrison?

HILL   Yes.

DR EMERSON   Tragic case . . . I hope you'll be able to get enough money for him to ease his mind.

HILL   Dr Emerson. It's not about that I wanted to see you. I thought I was coming about that, but Mr Harrison wishes to retain me to represent him on quite another matter.

DR EMERSON   Oh?

HILL   Yes, he wants to be discharged.

DR EMERSON   That's impossible.

HILL   Why?

DR EMERSON   To put it bluntly, he would die if we did that.

HILL   He knows that. It's what he wants.

DR EMERSON   And you are asking me to kill my patient?

HILL   I am representing Mr Harrison's wishes to you and asking for your reaction.

DR EMERSON   Well, you've had it. It's impossible. Now if that's really all you came about . . .

HILL   Dr Emerson, you can, of course, dismiss me like that if you choose to, but I would hardly think it serves anyone's interests, least of all Mr Harrison's.

DR EMERSON   I am trying to save Mr Harrison's life. There is no need to remind me of my duty to my patient, Mr Hill.

HILL   Or mine to my client, Dr Emerson.

DR EMERSON   . . . Are you telling me that you have accepted the job of coming to me to urge a course of action that will lose your client his life?

HILL   I hadn't accepted it . . . no . . . I told Mr Harrison I would talk to you first. Now I have and I begin to see why he thought it necessary to be represented.

DR EMERSON   Alright . . . Let's start again. Now tell me what you want to know.

HILL   Mr Harrison wishes to be discharged from hospital. Will you please make the necessary arrangements?

DR EMERSON No.

HILL May I ask why?

DR EMERSON Because Mr Harrison is incapable of living outside the hospital and it is my duty as a doctor to preserve life.

HILL I take it that Mr Harrison is a voluntary patient here.

DR EMERSON Of course.

HILL Then I fail to see the legal basis for your refusal.

DR EMERSON Can't you understand that Mr Harrison is suffering from depression? He is incapable of making a rational decision about his life and death.

HILL Are you maintaining that Mr Harrison is mentally unbalanced?

DR EMERSON Yes.

HILL Would you have any objection to my bringing in a psychiatrist for a second opinion?

DR EMERSON Of course not, but why not ask the consultant psychiatrist here? I'm sure he will be able to convince you.

HILL Has he examined Mr Harrison?

DR EMERSON No, but that can be quickly arranged.

HILL That's very kind of you, Dr Emerson, but I'm sure you'll understand if I ask for my own – whose opinion you are not sure of *before* he examines the patient.

DR EMERSON Good afternoon, Mr Hill.

HILL Good afternoon.

MR HILL *takes up his briefcase and leaves.*

DR EMERSON (*picks up the 'phone*): Could you find out where Dr Travers is please? I want to see him urgently, and put me through to the hospital secretary please. Well put me through when he's free.

Cross fade on KEN'S *room.*

The door opens and MR HILL *comes in.*

KEN Well, how was it on Olympus?

HILL Cloudy.

KEN No joy then?

HILL Dr Emerson does not wish to discharge you.

KEN Surprise, surprise. So what do we do now?

HILL Mr Harrison, I will be perfectly plain. Dr Emerson claims that you are not in a sufficiently healthy mental state to make a rational decision, especially one of this seriousness and finality. Now my position is, I am not competent to decide whether or not he is right.

KEN So how will you decide?

HILL I should like to have you examined by an independent psychiatrist and I will accept his view of the case and advise you accordingly.

KEN Fair enough. Will Dr Emerson agree?

HILL He has already. I ought to warn you that Dr Emerson is likely to take steps to have you admitted here as a person needing treatment under the Mental Health Act of 1959. This means that he can keep you here and give you what treatment he thinks fit.

KEN Can he do that?

HILL He probably can.

KEN Haven't I any say in this?

HILL Oh yes. He will need another signature and that doctor will have to be convinced that you ought compulsorily to be detained. Even if he agrees, we can appeal.

KEN Let's get on with it then.

HILL One thing at a time. First, you remember, our own psychiatrist.

KEN Wheel him in . . .

HILL   I'll be in touch soon then.

KEN   Oh, before you go. Yesterday I refused to take a
               tranquillizer and Dr Emerson came in and gave me
               an injection. It made me pretty dopey. If I was like
               that when the psychiatrist came, he'd lock me up for
               life!

HILL   I'll mention it to him. Goodbye for now then.

KEN   Goodbye.

               Cross fade on DR EMERSON'S *office.*

               DR EMERSON *is writing.* DR TRAVERS *knocks on his door
               and looks in.*

DR EMERSON Can you find me Dr Scott please?

               He puts the 'phone down.

DR TRAVERS You wanted to see me?

DR EMERSON Ah yes. If you can spare a moment.

DR TRAVERS What's the problem?

DR EMERSON Nasty one really. I have a road accident case,
               paralysed from the neck down. He's naturally very
               depressed and wants to discharge himself. But with a
               neurogenic bladder and all the rest of it, he couldn't
               last a week out of here. I need time to get him used
               to the idea.

DR TRAVERS How long ago was the accident?

DR EMERSON Six months.

DR TRAVERS A long time.

DR EMERSON Yes, well there were other injuries but we've just
               about got him physically stabilised. The trouble is
               that he's got himself a solicitor and if I am to keep
               him here, I'll have to admit him compulsorily under
               the Mental Health Act. I wondered if you'd see him.

DR TRAVERS I'll see him of course, but my signature won't help
               you.

DR EMERSON   Why not? You're the psychiatrist aren't you?

DR TRAVERS   Yes. But under the Act, you need two signatures and only one can come from a practitioner of the hospital where the patient is to be kept.

DR EMERSON   Bloody hell!

DR TRAVERS   Not to worry. I take it you regard this as an emergency.

DR EMERSON   Of course I do.

DR TRAVERS   Well, sign the application and then you've got three days to get another signature.

DR EMERSON   There'll be no problem about that surely?

DR TRAVERS   Depends upon whether he's clinically depressed or not.

DR EMERSON   You haven't understood. He's suicidal. He's determined to kill himself.

DR TRAVERS   I could name you several psychiatrists who wouldn't take that as evidence of insanity.

DR EMERSON   Well, I could name several psychiatrists who *are* evidence of insanity. I've had a lot of experience in this kind of case. I'm sure, absolutely sure, I can win him around, given time – a few months . . .

DR TRAVERS   I understand, Michael.

DR EMERSON   . . . So you'll look at him, will you? . . . And get another chap in? . . .

DR TRAVERS   Yes, I'll do that.

DR EMERSON   (*twinkling*): and . . . do me a favour, will you? Try and find an old codger like me, who believes in something better than suicide.

DR TRAVERS   (*grinning*): There's a chap at Ellertree . . . a very staunch Catholic, I believe. Would that suit you?

DR EMERSON   Be Jasus – sounds just the man!

DR TRAVERS   I'll see his notes and drop in on him . . .

DR EMERSON   Thank you very much Paul . . . I'm very grateful –
and Harrison will be too.

DR SCOTT *comes in the room.*

DR SCOTT   Oh, sorry.

DR TRAVERS   It's alright . . . I'm off . . . I'll see him then, Michael,
this afternoon.

DR TRAVERS *leaves.* DR SCOTT *looks at* DR EMERSON
questioningly.

DR SCOTT   You wanted me?

DR EMERSON   Ah yes. Harrison's decided to discharge himself.

DR SCOTT   Oh no, but I'm not surprised.

DR EMERSON   So, Travers is seeing him now.

DR SCOTT   Dr Travers won't make him change his mind.

DR EMERSON   I am committing him under Section 26.

DR SCOTT   Oh, will Dr Travers sign it?

DR EMERSON   Evidently if I do, he can't, but he knows a chap over
in Ellertree who probably will.

DR SCOTT   I see.

DR EMERSON   I have no choice, do you see Clare? He's got himself
a solicitor. It's the only way I can keep him here.

DR SCOTT   Are you sure you should?

DR EMERSON   Of course. No question.

DR SCOTT   It's his life.

DR EMERSON   But my responsibility.

DR SCOTT   Only if he's incapable of making his own
decision.

DR EMERSON   But he isn't capable. I refuse to believe that a
man with a mind as quick as his, a man with
enormous mental resources, would calmly choose
suicide.

DR SCOTT   But he has done just that.

DR EMERSON   And, therefore, I say he is unbalanced.

DR SCOTT   But surely a wish to die is not *necessarily* a symptom of insanity? A man might want to die for perfectly sane reasons.

DR EMERSON   No, Clare, a doctor cannot accept the choice for death; he's committed to life. When a patient is brought into my unit, he's in a bad way. I don't stand about thinking whether or not it's worth saving his life, I haven't the time for doubts. I get in there, do whatever I can to save life. I'm a doctor, not a judge.

DR SCOTT   I hope you will forgive me sir, for saying this, but I think that is just how you are behaving – as a judge.

DR EMERSON   You must, of course, say what you think – but I am the responsible person here.

DR SCOTT   I know that sir.

She makes to go.

DR EMERSON   I'm sure it's not necessary for me to say this but I'd rather there was no question of misunderstandings later . . . Mr Harrison is now physically stable. There is no reason why he should die; if he should die suddenly, I would think it necessary to order a post-mortem and to act on whatever was found.

DR SCOTT   . . . Mr Harrison is your patient sir.

DR EMERSON   (*smiling*): Of course, of course. You make that sound a fate worse than death.

DR SCOTT   Perhaps for him it is.

She goes out.

Cross fade on KEN'S *room.*

DR TRAVERS   Mr Harrison?

KEN   That's right.

DR TRAVERS	Dr Travers.
KEN	Are you a psychiatrist?
DR TRAVERS	Yes.
KEN	For or against me . . . Or does that sound like paranoia?
DR TRAVERS	You'd hardly expect me to make an instant diagnosis.
KEN	Did Dr Emerson send you?
DR TRAVERS	I work here, in the hospital.
KEN	Ah.
DR TRAVERS	Would you describe yourself as suffering from paranoia?
KEN	No.
DR TRAVERS	What would you say paranoia was?
KEN	Difficult. It depends on the person. A man whose feelings of security are tied to his own sense of what is right and can brook no denial. If he were, say, a sculptor, then he would describe his mental condition as paranoia. If, on the other hand, he was a doctor, we would describe it as professionalism.
DR TRAVERS	(*laughing*): You don't like doctors!
KEN	Do you like patients?
DR TRAVERS	Some.
KEN	I like some doctors.
DR TRAVERS	What's wrong with doctors then?
KEN	Speaking generally, I suppose that as a profession you've not learnt that the level of awareness of the population has risen dramatically; that black magic is no longer much use and that people *can* and *want* to understand what's wrong with them and many of them can make decisions about their own lives.
DR TRAVERS	What they need is information.
KEN	Of course, but as a rule, doctors dole out information

like a kosher butcher gives out pork sausages.

DR TRAVERS That's fair. But you'd agree that patients need medical knowledge to make good decisions?

KEN I would. Look at me, for example. I'm a sculptor, an airy-fairy artist, with no real hard knowledge and no capability to understand anything about my body. You're a doctor but I think I would hold my own with a competition in anatomy with *you*.

DR TRAVERS It's a long time since I did my anatomy.

KEN Of course. Whereas I was teaching it every day up to six months ago. It wouldn't be fair.

DR TRAVERS Your knowledge of anatomy may be excellent, but what's your neurology like, or your dermatology, endocrinology, urology and so on.

KEN Lousy, and in so far as these bear on my case, I should be grateful for information so that I can make a proper decision. But it is my decision. If you came to my studio to buy something, and look at all my work, and you say: 'I want that bronze' and I say to you: 'Look, you don't know anything about sculpture. The proportion of that is all wrong, the texture is boring and it should have been made in wood anyway. You are having the marble!' You'd think I was nuts. If you were sensible you'd ask for my professional opinion but if you were a mature adult, you'd reserve the right to choose for yourself.

DR TRAVERS But we're not talking about a piece of sculpture to decorate a room, but about your life.

KEN That's right Doctor. *My* life.

DR TRAVERS But your obvious intelligence weakens your case. I'm not saying that you would find life easy but you do have resources that an unintelligent person doesn't have.

KEN That sounds like Catch 22. If you're clever and sane enough to put up an invincible case for suicide, it demonstrates you ought not to die.

DR TRAVERS *moves the stool near the bed.*

KEN That's a disturbing tidiness compulsion you've got there.

DR TRAVERS I was an only child; enough of me. Having any relationships outside the hospital? You're not married I see.

KEN No, thank God.

DR TRAVERS A girl friend?

KEN A fiancée actually. I asked her not to visit me any more. About a fortnight ago.

DR TRAVERS She must have been upset.

KEN Better that than a lifetime's sacrifice.

DR TRAVERS She wanted to . . . stay with you then?

KEN Oh yes . . . Had it all worked out . . . But she's a young healthy woman. She wants babies – real ones. Not ones that never *will* learn to walk.

DR TRAVERS But if that's what she really wants.

KEN Oh come on Doctor. If that's what she really wants, there's plenty of other cripples who want help. I told her to go to release her, I hope, from the guilt she would feel if she did what she really wanted to.

DR TRAVERS That's very generous.

KEN Balls. Really, Doctor, I did it for *me.* It would destroy *my* self-respect if I allowed myself to become the object with which people can safely exploit their masochist tendencies.

DR TRAVERS That's putting it very strongly.

KEN Yes. Too strong. But you are beginning to sound like the chaplain. He was in here the other day. He seemed to think I should be quite happy to be God's chosen vessel into which people could pour their compassion . . . That it was alright being a cripple because it made other folk feel good when they helped me.

DR TRAVERS What about your parents?

KEN Working class folk – they live in Scotland. I thought it would break my mother – I always thought of my father as a very tough egg. But it was the other way round. My father can only think with his hands. He used to stand around here – completely at a loss. My mother would sit here – just understanding. She knows what suffering's about. They were here a week ago – I got rid of my father for a while and told my mother what I was going to do. She looked at me for a minute. There were tears in her eyes. She said: 'Aye lad, it's thy life . . . don't worry about your dad – I'll get him over it' . . . She stood up and I said: 'What about you' 'What about me?' she said, 'Do you think life's so precious to me, I'm frightened of dying?' . . . I'd like to think I was my mother's son.

DR TRAVERS . . . Yes, well, we shall have to see . . .

KEN What about? You mean you haven't made up your mind?

DR TRAVERS I shall have to do some tests . . .

KEN What tests for Christ's sake? I can tell you now, my time over a hundred metres is lousy.

DR TRAVERS You seem very angry.

KEN Of course I'm angry . . . No, no . . . I'm . . . Yes. I am angry. (*breathing*) But I am trying to hold it in because you'll just write me off as in a manic phase of a manic depressive cycle.

DR TRAVERS You are very free with psychiatric jargon.

KEN Oh well then, you'll be able to say I'm an obsessive hypochondriac. (*breathing*)

DR TRAVERS   I certainly wouldn't do that Mr Harrison.

KEN   Can't you see what a trap I am in? Can anyone prove that they are sane? Could you?

DR TRAVERS   . . . I'll come and see you again.

KEN   No, don't come and see me again, because every time you come I'll get more and more angry, and more and more upset and depressed. And eventually you will have destroyed my mind.

DR TRAVERS   I'm sorry if I upset you Mr Harrison.

DR TRAVERS *replaces the stool and exits. He crosses to the* SISTER'S *office. Enter* DR SCOTT *and* MR HILL.

DR SCOTT   I hate the idea. It's against all my training and instincts . . .

HILL   Mine too. But in this case, we're not dealing with euthanasia are we?

DR SCOTT   Something very close.

HILL   No. Something very far away. Suicide.

DR SCOTT   Thank you for a lovely meal.

HILL   Not at all, I am glad you accepted. Tell me, what would you think, or rather feel, if there was a miracle and Mr Harrison was granted the use of his arms for just one minute and he used them to grab a bottle of sleeping tablets and swallowed the lot?

DR SCOTT   . . . It's irrational but . . . I'd be very . . . relieved.

HILL   It wouldn't go against your instincts? . . . You wouldn't feel it was a wasted life and fight with stomach pumps and all that?

DR SCOTT   No . . . not if it was my decision.

HILL   You might even be sure there *was* a bottle of tablets handy and you not there.

DR SCOTT   You make it harder and harder . . . but yes, I might do that . . .

HILL   Yes. Perhaps we ought to make suicide respectable again. Whenever anyone kills himself there's a whole legal rigmarole to go through – investigations, inquests and so on – and it all seems designed to find someone or something to *blame*. Can you ever recall a coroner saying something like: 'We've heard all the evidence of how John Smith was facing literally insuperable odds and he made a courageous decision. I record a verdict of a noble death?'

DR SCOTT   No . . . It's been a . . . very pleasant evening.

HILL   Thank you. For me too.

DR SCOTT   I don't know if I've helped you though.

HILL   You have. I've made up my mind.

DR SCOTT   You'll help him?

HILL   Yes . . . I hope you're not sorry.

DR SCOTT   I'm pleased . . .

HILL   I'm sure it is morally wrong for anyone to try to hand the responsibility for their death to anyone else. And it's wrong to accept that responsibility, but Ken isn't trying to do that.

DR SCOTT   I'm glad you've made up your mind . . . Good-night.

They stop.

HILL   I hope I see you again.

DR SCOTT   I'm on the 'phone . . . Goodnight.

They exit. NURSE SADLER *goes into* KEN'S *room with a meal.*

KEN   You still on duty?

NURSE   We're very short-staffed . . .

She prepares to feed KEN *with a spoon.*

NURSE It looks good tonight . . . Minced beef.

KEN Excellent . . . and what wine shall we order then? How about a '48 claret? Yes, I think so . . . Send for the wine waiter.

NURSE You are a fool Mr Harrison.

KEN Is there any reason why I shouldn't have wine?

NURSE I don't know. I'll ask Sister if you like . . .

KEN After all, the hospital seems determined to depress my consciousness. But they'd probably think it's immoral if I enjoy it.

NURSE SADLER *gives him a spoonful of mince.*

KEN It's a bit salty.

NURSE Do you want some water?

KEN That would be good. Very nice . . . Not too full of body. Château Ogston Reservoir, I think, with just a cheeky little hint of Jeyes fluid from the steriliser.

NURSE We use Milton.

KEN Oh dear . . . you'd better add to my notes. The final catastrophe. Mr Harrison's palate is failing; rush up the emergency taste resuscitation unit. (*In a phoney American accent*) 'Nurse, give me orange . . . No response . . . Quick the lemon . . . God! Not a flicker . . . We're on the tightrope . . . Nurse pass the ultimate . . . Quick, there's no time to lose . . . Pass the hospital mince.' That would bring people back from the dead. Don't tell Emerson that or he'll try it. I don't want any more of that.

NURSE SADLER *exits.* DR SCOTT *comes in.*

KEN Sister.

DR SCOTT No, it's me. Still awake?

KEN Yes.

DR SCOTT   It's late.

KEN   What time is it?

DR SCOTT   Half past eleven.

KEN   The Night Sister said I could have the light for half an hour. I couldn't sleep. I wanted to think.

DR SCOTT   Yes.

KEN   You look lovely.

DR SCOTT   Thank you.

KEN   Have you been out?

DR SCOTT   For a meal.

KEN   Nice. Good company?

DR SCOTT   You're fishing.

KEN   That's right.

DR SCOTT   Yes, it was good company.

KEN   A colleague?

DR SCOTT   No. Actually it was Philip Hill, your solicitor.

KEN   Well, well, well . . . The randy old devil. He didn't take long to get cracking did he?

DR SCOTT   It was just a dinner.

KEN   I know I engaged him to act for me. I didn't realise he would see his duties so comprehensively.

DR SCOTT   It was just dinner!

KEN   Well, I hope my surrogate self behaved myself.

DR SCOTT   You were a perfect gentlemen.

KEN   Mm . . . then perhaps I'd better engage another surrogate.

DR SCOTT   Do you mind really?

KEN   . . . No. Unless you convinced him that Emerson was right.

DR SCOTT   . . . I didn't try.

KEN   Thank you.

DR SCOTT   I think you are enjoying all this.

KEN   I suppose I am in a way. For the first time in six months I feel like a human being again.

DR SCOTT   Yes.

        A pause.

DR SCOTT   Isn't that the whole point, Ken, that . . .

KEN   You called me Ken.

DR SCOTT   Do you mind?

KEN   Oh! No, I liked it. I'll just chalk it up as another credit for today.

DR SCOTT   I was saying, isn't that just the point, isn't that what this fight has shown you? That you are a human being again. You're not fighting for death. I don't think you want to win.

KEN   That was what I had to think about.

DR SCOTT   And have you . . . changed your mind?

KEN   . . . No. I know I'm enjoying the fight and I had to be sure that I wanted to win, really get what I'm fighting for, and not just doing it to convince myself I'm still alive.

DR SCOTT   And are you sure?

KEN   Yes, quite sure, for me life is over. I want it recognised because I can't do the things that I want to do. That means I can't say the things I want to say. Is that a better end? You understand don't you?

        NURSE SADLER *comes in with a feeding cup.*

NURSE   I didn't know you were here, Doctor.

DR SCOTT   Yes, I'm just going.

KEN   See what I mean, Doctor. Here is my substitute mum, with her porcelain pap. This isn't for me.

DR SCOTT   No . . .

KEN   So tomorrow, on with the fight!

DR SCOTT   Goodnight . . . and good luck.

Fade.

KERSHAW So our psychiatrist is prepared to state that Harrison is sane.

HILL Yes, he was sure. I'll have his written report tomorrow. He said he could understand the hospital fighting to save their patient from himself, but no matter how much he sympathised with them and how much he wished he could get Harrison to change his mind, nevertheless, he was sane and knew exactly what he was doing and why he was doing it.

KERSHAW And you say that the hospital are holding him here under Section 26.

HILL Yes, they rang me this morning. They got another chap in from Ellertree to sign it as well as Emerson.

KERSHAW Hm . . . Tricky. There's no precedent for this you know. Fascinating.

HILL Yes.

KERSHAW And you're sure in your mind he knows what he's doing?

HILL Yes.

KERSHAW . . . Well . . . Let's see him, shall we?

HILL Here's the Sister's office.

KERSHAW Is she your standard gorgon?

HILL Only on the outside. But under that iron surface beats a heart of stainless steel.

They go into SISTER'S *office.*

HILL Good morning Sister.

SISTER Morning Mr Hill.

HILL This is a colleague, Mr Kershaw.

SISTER Good morning.

KERSHAW Good morning.

HILL   Is it alright to see Mr Harrison? . . .

SISTER Have you asked Dr Emerson? . . .

HILL   Oh yes . . . before we came . . .

SISTER I see . . .

HILL   You can check with him . . .

SISTER . . . I don't think that's necessary . . . However, I'm afraid I shall have to ask you if I can stay with Mr Harrison whilst you interview him.

HILL   Why?

SISTER We are all very worried about Mr Harrison's mental condition as you know. Twice recently he has . . . got excited . . . and his breathing function has not been able to cope with the extra demands. Dr Emerson has ordered that at any time Mr Harrison is subjected to stress, someone must be there as a precaution.

HILL   . . . I see.

He glances at MR KERSHAW, *who shrugs.*

HILL   Very well.

SISTER This way, gentlemen.

They go into KEN'S *room.*

HILL   Good morning Mr Harrison.

KEN   Morning.

HILL   I've brought along Mr Kershaw. He is the barrister who is advising us.

KERSHAW Good morning Mr Harrison.

HILL   Your doctor has insisted that Sister remains with us – to see you don't get too excited.

KEN   Oh! Sister, you know very well that your very presence always excites me tremendously. It must be the white apron and black stockings. A perfect mixture of mother and mistress.

SISTER *grins sheepishly and takes a seat at the head of the bed.* KEN *strains his head to look at her.* SISTER *turns back the covers.*

KEN Sister, what are you doing! Oh. Just for a minute there, Sister . . .

SISTER *takes his pulse.*

HILL . . . Well . . .

SISTER Just a moment, Mr Hill . . .

She finishes taking his pulse.

SISTER Very well.

KEN So, Mr Kershaw, what is your advice?

MR KERSHAW *pauses.* MR HILL *makes to speak but* MR KERSHAW *stops him with a barely perceptible shake of the head. A longer pause.*

KERSHAW . . . If you succeed in your aim you will be dead within a week.

KEN I know.

KERSHAW . . . I am informed that without a catheter the toxic substance will build up in your bloodstream and you will be slowly poisoned by your own blood.

KEN (*smiles*): . . . You should have brought along a tape-recorder. That speech would be much more dramatic with sound effects!

KERSHAW (*relaxing and smiling*): I had to be sure you know what you are doing.

KEN I know.

KERSHAW And you have no doubt whatsoever; no slightest reservations? . . .

KEN None at all.

KERSHAW Let's look at the possibilities. You are now being held under the Mental Health Act Section 26, which means they can keep you here and give you any treatment they believe you need. Under the law we can appeal to a tribunal.

KEN How long will that take?

KERSHAW . . . Up to a year.

KEN A year! Oh God, can't it be quicker than that?

KERSHAW It might be quicker, but it could be a year.

KEN Jesus Christ! I really would be crazy in a year.

KERSHAW That's procedure.

KEN I couldn't stay like this for another year, I couldn't.

HILL We could always try habeas corpus.

KERSHAW That would depend if we could find someone.

KEN Habeas corpus? What's that? I thought it was something to do with criminals.

KERSHAW Well, it usually is, Mr Harrison. Briefly, it's against the law to deprive anyone of their liberty without proper cause. If anyone is so deprived, they or a friend can apply for a writ of habeas corpus, which is the Latin for 'you may have the body'.

KEN Particularly apt in my case.

KERSHAW . . . The people who are doing the detaining have to produce the . . . person, before the judge and if they can't give a good enough reason for keeping him, the judge will order that he be released.

KEN It sounds as if it will take as long as that tribunal you were talking about.

KERSHAW No. Habeas corpus is one of the few legal processes that move very fast. We can approach any judge at any time even when the courts aren't sitting and he will see that it's heard straight away – in a day or so usually.

HILL   If you could find a judge to hear it.

KEN   Why shouldn't a judge hear it?

KERSHAW   Habeas corpus itself is fairly rare. This would be rarer.

KEN   Will I have to go to court?

KERSHAW   I doubt it. The hearing can be in court or in private, in the Judge's Chambers as we say. The best thing to do in this case is for Mr Hill and I to find a judge, issue the write, then I'll get together with the hospital's barrister and we'll approach the judge together and suggest we hold the subsequent hearing here.

KEN   In this room?

KERSHAW   I expect the judge will agree. If he ordered you to be produced in court and anything happened to you, it would be a classical case of prejudging the issue.

KEN   I wouldn't mind.

KERSHAW   But the judge would feel rather foolish. I should think it would be in a few days.

KEN   Thank you. It will be an unusual case for you – making a plea for a defendant's death.

KERSHAW   I'll be honest with you. It's a case I could bear to lose.

KEN   If you do – it's a life sentence for me.

KERSHAW   Well, we shall see. Good morning Mr Harrison.

They go out with the SISTER. *They pause at the* SISTER'S *office.*

HILL   Thank you very much, Sister . . . I'm very sorry about all this. I do realise it must be upsetting for you.

SISTER   Not at all Mr Hill. As I have a stainless steel heart, it's easy to keep it sterilised of emotion. Good morning.

She goes into her room. HILL *and* KERSHAW *go out.*

Cross fade on KEN'S *room.*

JOHN *and* NURSE SADLER *are setting chairs for the hearing.* JOHN *beings to sing 'Dry Bones'.*

NURSE   John!

JOHN   What's the matter?

NURSE SADLER *is confused.*

NURSE   Nothing of course . . . silly . . .

KEN *picks up the vibes between the two.*

KEN   Hello, hello . . . What have we here? Don't tell me that Cupid has donned his antiseptic gown and is flying the corridors of the hospital, shooting his hypodermic syringes into maidens' hearts . . .

NURSE   No!

KEN   John?

JOHN   Honestly, your honour, I'm not guilty. I was just walking down the corridor when I was struck dumb by the beauty of this nurse.

NURSE   Don't be an idiot John . . . We need an extra chair . . . Can you go and find one please?

JOHN   Your wishes, oh queen, are my command.

He bows and goes out.

NURSE   He is a fool.

KEN   He isn't. He's been bloody good to me. Have you been out with him? . . . It's none of my business of course.

NURSE   We went to a club of his last night . . . He plays in a band you know.

KEN   Yes, I know.

NURSE   They're really good. They should go a long

way . . . Still, I shouldn't be going on like this.

KEN Why not? . . . Because I'm paralysed? Because I can't go dancing?

NURSE Well . . .

KEN The other day I was low and said to John, who was shaving me, I was useless, what could I do? I served no purpose and all the rest of the whining miseries. John set about finding things I could do. He said first, because I could move my head from side to side (KEN *does so*). I could be a tennis umpire; then as my head was going, I could knock a pendulum from side to side and keep a clock going. Then he said I could be a child-minder and because kids were always doing what they shouldn't I could be perpetually shaking my head. He went on and on getting more and more fantastic – like radar scanners. I laughed so much that the Sister had to rush in and give me oxygen.

NURSE He is funny.

KEN He's more than that. He's free!

NURSE Free?

KEN Free of guilt. Most everybody here feels guilt about me – including you. That's why you didn't want to tell me what a fantastic time you had dancing. So everybody makes me feel worse because I make them feel guilty. But not John. He's sorry for me but knows bloody well it isn't his fault. He's a tonic.

JOHN *comes back carrying* SISTER'S *armchair.*

NURSE John! Did Sister say you could have that chair?

JOHN She wasn't there . . .

NURSE She'll kill you; no-one ever sits in her chair.

JOHN Why? Is it contaminated or something? I just thought that if the poor old Judge had to sit here listening to that

miserable bugger moaning on about wanting to die,
the least we could do was to make him comfortable.

KEN (*laughing to* NURSE SADLER): See?

JOHN *sits in the chair and assumes a grave face.*

JOHN Now, this is a very serious case. The two charges are
proved . . . Firstly, this hospital has been found
guilty of using drugs to make people happy. That's
terrible. Next and most surprisingly of all, this
hospital, in spite of all their efforts to the contrary,
are keeping people alive! We can't have that.

Footsteps outside.

NURSE Sister's coming!

JOHN *jumps up and stands between the chair and the
door.* SISTER *comes in and as she approaches the bed
with her back to the chair,* JOHN *slips out of the room.*

KEN Well now, we have some very important visitors
today Sister.

SISTER Indeed we have.

KEN Will you be here?

SISTER No.

KEN I feel a bit like a traitor.

SISTER . . . We all do what we've got to.

KEN That's right, but not all of us do it as well as you
Sister . . .

SISTER (*quickly*): . . . Thank you.

She moves quickly to go. DR SCOTT *comes in.*

DR SCOTT Good morning Sister.

SISTER (*brightly*): Good morning.

She goes quickly without noticing the chair. DR SCOTT *watches her go.*

KEN   I've upset her I'm afraid.

DR SCOTT You shouldn't do that. She is a marvellous Sister. You ought to see some of the others.

KEN   That's what I told her.

DR SCOTT Oh, I see. Well, I should think that's just about the one way past her defences. How are you this morning?

KEN   Fine.

DR SCOTT And you're going ahead with it?

KEN   Of course.

DR SCOTT Of course.

KEN   I haven't had any tablets, yesterday or today.

DR SCOTT No.

KEN   Thank you.

DR SCOTT Thank the Judge. He ordered it.

KEN   Ah!

DR EMERSON *comes in.*

DR EMERSON Good morning Mr Harrison.

KEN   Morning Doctor.

DR EMERSON There's still time.

KEN   No, I want to go on with it . . . unless you'll discharge me.

DR EMERSON I'm afraid I can't do that. The Judge and lawyers are conferring. I thought I'd just pop along and see if you were alright. We've made arrangements for the witnesses to wait in the Sister's office. I am one, so I should be grateful if you would remain here, with Mr Harrison.

DR SCOTT Of course.

DR EMERSON Well I don't want to meet the Judge before I have to. I wish you the best of luck Mr Harrison, so that we'll be able to carry on treating you.

KEN (*smiling*): Thank you for your good wishes.

DR EMERSON *nods and goes out.*

DR SCOTT If I didn't know *you* I'd say *he* was the most obstinate man I've ever met.

As DR EMERSON *makes for his office,* MR HILL *comes down the corridor.*

HILL Good morning.

DR EMERSON Morning.

MR HILL *stops and calls after* DR EMERSON.

HILL Oh, Dr Emerson . . .

DR EMERSON Yes?

HILL I don't know . . . I just want to say how sorry I am that you have been forced into such a . . . distasteful situation.

DR EMERSON It's not over yet Mr Hill. I have every confidence that the law is not such an ass that it will force me to watch a patient of mine die unnecessarily.

HILL We are just as confident that the law is not such an ass that it will allow anyone arbitrary power.

DR EMERSON My power isn't arbitrary; I've earned it with knowledge and skill and it's also subject to the laws of nature.

HILL And to the laws of the state.

DR EMERSON If the state is so foolish as to believe it is competent to judge a purely professional issue.

HILL It's always doing that. Half the civil cases in the calendar arise because someone is challenging a professional's opinion.

DR EMERSON   I don't know about other professions but I do know this one, medicine, is being seriously threatened because of the intervention of law. Patients are becoming so litigious that doctors will soon be afraid to offer any opinion or take any action at all.

HILL   Then they will be sued for negligence.

DR EMERSON   We can't win.

HILL   Everybody wins. You wouldn't like to find yourself powerless in the hands of, say, a lawyer or a . . . bureaucrat. I wouldn't like to find myself powerless in the hands of a doctor.

DR EMERSON   You make me sound as if I were some sort of Dracula . . .

HILL   No! . . . I for one certainly don't doubt your good faith but in spite of that I wouldn't like to place *anyone* above the law.

DR EMERSON   I don't want to be above the law; I just want to be under laws that take full account of professional opinion.

HILL   I'm sure it will do that Dr Emerson. The question is, whose professional opinion?

DR EMERSON   We shall see.

    MR ANDREW EDEN, *the hospital's barrister, and* MR HILL *and* MR KERSHAW *come into* KEN'S *room.*

HILL   Morning Mr Harrison. This is Mr Eden who will be representing the hospital.

KEN   Hello.

    They settle themselves into the chairs. The SISTER *enters with the* JUDGE.

SISTER   Mr Justice Millhouse.

JUDGE	Mr Kenneth Harrison?
KEN	Yes my Lord.
JUDGE	This is an informal hearing which I want to keep as brief as possible. You are, I take it, Dr Scott?
DR SCOTT	Yes my Lord.
JUDGE	I should be grateful Doctor, if you would interrupt the proceedings at any time you think it necessary.
DR SCOTT	Yes my Lord.
JUDGE	I have decided in consultation with Mr Kershaw and Mr Hill that we shall proceed thus. I will hear a statement from Dr Michael Emerson as to why he believes Mr Harrison is legally detained, and then a statement from Dr Richard Barr, who will support the application. We have decided not to subject Mr Harrison to examination and cross-examination.
KEN	But I . . .
JUDGE	(*sharply*): Just a moment Mr Harrison. If, as appears likely, there remains genuine doubt as to the main issue, I shall question Mr Harrison myself. Dr Scott, I wonder if you would ask Dr Emerson to come in.
DR SCOTT	Yes my Lord.

She goes out.

DR SCOTT	Would you come in now sir.

SISTER *and* DR EMERSON *come into* KEN's *room.*

JUDGE	Dr Emerson, I would like you to take the oath.

The JUDGE *hands* DR EMERSON *a card with the oath written on it.*

DR EMERSON	I swear the evidence that I give shall be the truth, the whole truth and nothing but the truth.
KERSHAW	Stand over there please.

The JUDGE *nods to* MR EDEN.

EDEN   You are Dr Michael Emerson?

DR EMERSON   I am.

EDEN   And what is your position here?

DR EMERSON   I am a consultant physician and in charge of the intensive care unit.

EDEN   Dr Emerson, would you please give a brief account of your treatment of this patient.

DR EMERSON   (*referring to notes*): Mr Harrison was admitted here on the afternoon of October 9th, as an emergency following a road accident. He was suffering from a fractured left tibia, and right tibia and fibia, a fractured pelvis, four fractured ribs, one of which had punctured the lung, and a dislocated fourth vertebra, which had ruptured the spinal cord. He was extensively bruised and had minor lacerations. He was deeply unconscious and remained so for thirty hours. As a result of treatment all the broken bones and ruptured tissue have healed with the exception of a severed spinal cord and this, together with a mental trauma, is now all that remains of the initial injury.

EDEN   Precisely, Doctor. Let us deal with those last two points. The spinal cord. Will there be any further improvements in that?

DR EMERSON   In the present state of medical knowledge, I would think not.

EDEN   And the mental trauma you spoke of?

DR EMERSON   It's impossible to injure the body to the extent that Mr Harrison did and not affect the mind. It is common in these cases that depression and the tendency to make wrong decisions goes on for months, even years.

EDEN   And in your view Mr Harrison is suffering from such a depression?

DR EMERSON Yes.

EDEN Thank you Doctor.

JUDGE Mr Kershaw?

KERSHAW Doctor. Is there any objective way you could demonstrate this trauma? Are there, for example, the results of any tests, or any measurements you can take to show how it is?

DR EMERSON No.

KERSHAW Then how do you distinguish between a medical syndrome and a sane, even justified, depression?

DR EMERSON By using my thirty years' experience as a physician, dealing with both types.

KERSHAW No more questions my Lord.

JUDGE Mr Eden do you wish to re-examine?

EDEN No my Lord.

JUDGE Thank you Doctor. Would you ask Dr Barr if he would step in please?

DR EMERSON *goes out.*

DR EMERSON It's you now Barr.

SISTER *brings* DR BARR *into* KEN'S *room.*

SISTER Dr Barr.

JUDGE Dr Barr, will you take the oath please.

He does so.

JUDGE Mr Kershaw.

KERSHAW You are Dr Richard Barr?

DR BARR I am.

KERSHAW And what position do you hold?

DR BARR I am a consultant psychiatrist at Norwood Park Hospital.

KERSHAW   That is primarily a mental hospital is it not?

DR BARR   It is.

KERSHAW   Then you must see a large number of patients suffering from depressive illness.

DR BARR   I do, yes.

KERSHAW   You have examined Mr Harrison?

DR BARR   I have, yes.

KERSHAW   Would you say that he was suffering from such an illness?

DR BARR   No, I would not.

KERSHAW   Are you quite sure Doctor?

DR BARR   Yes, I am.

KERSHAW   The court has heard evidence that Mr Harrison is depressed. Would you dispute that?

DR BARR   No, but depression is not necessarily an illness. I would say that Mr Harrison's depression is reactive rather than endogenous. That is to say, he is reacting in a perfectly rational way to a very bad situation.

KERSHAW   Thank you Dr Barr.

JUDGE   Mr Eden?

EDEN   Dr Barr. Are there any objective results that you could produce to prove Mr Harrison is capable?

DR BARR   There are clinical symptoms of endogenous depression, of course, disturbed sleep patterns, loss of appetite, lasitude, but, even if they were present, they would be masked by the physical condition.

EDEN   So how can you be sure this *is* in fact just a reactive depression?

DR BARR   Just by experience, that's all, and by discovering when I talk to him that he has a remarkably incisive mind and is perfectly capable of understanding his position and of deciding what to do about it.

EDEN   One last thing Doctor; do you think Mr Harrison has made the right decision?

KERSHAW (*quickly*): Is that really relevant my Lord? After all . . .

JUDGE Not really . . .

DR BARR I should like to answer it though.

JUDGE Very well.

DR BARR No, I thought he made the wrong decision. (*to* KEN) Sorry.

EDEN No more questions my Lord.

JUDGE Do you wish to re-examine, Mr Kershaw?

KERSHAW No thank you my Lord.

JUDGE That will be all Dr Barr.

DR BARR *goes out. The* JUDGE *stands.*

JUDGE Do you feel like answering some questions?

KEN Of course.

JUDGE Thank you.

KEN You are too kind.

JUDGE Not at all.

KEN I mean it. I'd prefer it if you were a hanging judge.

JUDGE There aren't any any more.

KEN Society is now much more sensitive and humane?

JUDGE You could put it that way.

KEN I'll settle for that.

JUDGE I would like you to take the oath. Dr Scott, his right hand please.

KEN *takes the oath.*

JUDGE The consultant physician here has given evidence that you are not capable of making a rational decision.

KEN He's wrong.

JUDGE Why then do you think he came to that opinion?

KEN He's a good doctor and won't let a patient die if he can help it.

JUDGE He found that you were suffering from acute depression.

KEN Is that surprising? I am almost totally paralysed. I'd be insane if I *weren't* depressed.

JUDGE But there is a difference between being unhappy and being depressed in the medical sense.

KEN I would have thought that my psychiatrist answered that point.

JUDGE But, surely, wishing to die must be strong evidence that the depression has moved beyond a mere unhappiness into a medical realm?

KEN I don't wish to die.

JUDGE Then what is this case all about?

KEN Nor do I wish to live at any price. Of course I want to live but as far as I am concerned, I'm dead already. I merely require the doctors to recognise the fact. I cannot accept this condition constitutes life in any real sense at all.

JUDGE Certainly, you're alive legally.

KEN I think I could challenge even that.

JUDGE How?

KEN Any reasonable definition of life must include the idea of its being self-supporting. I seem to remember something in the papers – when all the heart transplant controversy was on – about it being alright to take someone's heart if they require constant attention from respirators and so on to keep them alive.

JUDGE There also has to be absolutely no brain activity at all. Yours is certainly working.

KEN It is and sanely.

JUDGE That is the question to be decided.

KEN My Lord, I am not asking anyone to kill me. I am only asking to be discharged from this hospital.

JUDGE It comes to the same thing.

KEN Then that proves my point; not just the fact that I will spend the rest of my life in hospital, but that whilst I am here, everything is geared just to keeping my brain active, with no real possibility of it ever being able to direct anything. As far as I can see, that is an act of deliberate cruelty.

JUDGE Surely, it would be more cruel if society let people die, when it could, with some effort, keep them alive.

KEN No, not *more* cruel, *just* as cruel.

JUDGE Then why should the hospital let you die – if it is just as cruel?

KEN The cruelty doesn't reside in saving someone or allowing them to die. It resides in the fact that the choice is removed from the man concerned.

JUDGE But a man who is very desperately depressed is not capable of making a reasonable choice.

KEN As you said, my Lord, that is the question to be decided.

JUDGE Alright. You tell me why it is a reasonable choice that you decide to die.

KEN It is a question of dignity. Look at me here. I can do nothing, not even the basic primitive functions. I cannot even urinate, I have a permanent catheter attached to me. Every few days my bowels are washed out. Every few hours two nurses have to turn me over or I would rot away from bedsores. Only my brain functions unimpaired but even that is futile because I can't act on any conclusions it comes to. This hearing proves that. Will you please listen.

JUDGE I am listening.

KEN I choose to acknowledge the fact that I am in fact dead and I find the hospital's persistent effort to maintain this shadow of life an indignity and it's inhumane.

JUDGE But wouldn't you agree that many people with appalling physical handicaps have overcome them and lived essentially creative, dignified lives?

KEN Yes, I would, but the dignity starts with their choice. If I choose to live, it would be appalling if society killed me. If I choose to die, it is equally appalling if society keeps me alive.

JUDGE I cannot accept that it is undignified for society to devote resources to keeping someone alive. Surely it enhances that society.

KEN It is not undignified if the man wants to stay alive, but I must restate that the dignity starts with his choice. Without it, it is degrading because technology has taken over from human will. My Lord, if I cannot be a man, I do not wish to be a medical achievement. I'm fine . . . I am fine.

JUDGE It's alright. I have no more questions.

The JUDGE *stands up and walks to the window. He thinks a moment.*

JUDGE This is a most unusual case. Before I make a judgement I want to state that I believe all the parties have acted in good faith. I propose to consider this for a moment. The law on this is fairly clear. A deliberate decision to embark on a course of action that will lead inevitably to death is not *ipso facto* evidence to insanity. If it were, society would have to reward many men with a dishonourable burial rather than a posthumous medal for gallantry. On the other hand, we do have to bear in mind that Mr Harrison has suffered massive physical injuries and it is possible that his mind is affected. Any

judge in his career will have met men who are
without doubt insane in the meaning of the Act
and yet appear in the witness box to be rational.
We must, in this case, be most careful not to allow
Mr Harrison's obvious wit and intelligence to blind
us to the fact that he could be suffering from a
depressive illness . . . and so we have to face the
disturbing fact of the divided evidence . . . and bear
in mind that, however much we may sympathise
with Mr Harrison in his cogently argued case to be
allowed to die, the law instructs us to ignore it if it is
the product of a disturbed or clinically depressed
mind . . . However, I am satisfied that Mr Harrison is
a brave and cool man who is in complete control of
his faculties and I shall therefore make an order for
him to be set free.

A pause. The JUDGE *walks over to* KEN.

JUDGE   Well you got your hanging judge!

KEN   I think not my Lord. Thank you.

The JUDGE *nods and smiles.*

JUDGE   Goodbye.

He turns and goes. He meets DR EMERSON *in the*
SISTER'S *room. Whilst he talks to him everyone else,*
except DR SCOTT, *comes out.*

JUDGE   Ah Dr Emerson.

DR EMERSON   My Lord?

JUDGE   I'm afraid you'll have to release your patient.

DR EMERSON   I see.

JUDGE   I'm sorry. I understand how you must feel.

DR EMERSON   Thank you.

JUDGE   If ever I have to have a road accident, I hope it's in this town and I finish up here.

DR EMERSON Thank you again.

JUDGE Goodbye.

He walks down the corridor. DR EMERSON *stands a moment then slowly goes back to the room.* KEN *is looking out of the window.* DR SCOTT *is sitting by the bed.*

DR EMERSON Where will you go?

KEN I'll get a room somewhere.

DR EMERSON There's no need.

KEN Don't let's . . .

DR EMERSON We'll stop treatment, remove the drips. Stop feeding you if you like. You'll be unconscious in three days, dead in six at most.

KEN There'll be no last minute resuscitation?

DR EMERSON Only with your express permission.

KEN That's very kind; why are you doing it?

DR EMERSON Simple! You might change your mind.

KEN *smiles and shakes his head.*

KEN Thanks. I won't change my mind, but I'd like to stay.

DR EMERSON *nods and goes.* DR SCOTT *stands and moves to the door. She turns and moves to* KEN *as if to kiss him.*

KEN Oh, don't, but thank you.

DR SCOTT *smiles weakly and goes out.*

The lights are held for a long moment and then snap out.

THE END

QUESTIONS AND EXPLORATIONS

1 Keeping Track

A series of questions, for discussion or writing, to keep track of characters, themes and issues as the play progresses. You might use these as a basis for a 'journal' of your responses to what you read, or you might use groups of questions as the basis for coursework assignments.

Act One

1 What do you learn about Ken's injuries in the opening moments of the play?
2 Ken calls the hospital staff 'the optimism industry'. Does the optimism seem to be working on him? (What do his jokes with the nurses tell you about his state of mind?)
3 What does Ken mean by 'the monstrous regiment'?
4 Ken calls Nurse Sadler 'a breath of fresh air'. What differences do you see between the new nurse and the Sister?
5 Ken says that he is feeling sorry for himself this morning. Is there any evidence to support this comment, or do you think he is feeling something else altogether?
6 Why is Ken 'a little agitated this morning'?
7 How does Ken define 'being professional'? Does his definition seem to you to fit what you have seen of the medical staff so far in the play?
8 What are Ken's views on the purpose of tranquillizers?
9 Why does Ken refuse the tranquillizer?
10 Why does John, the orderly, not take this hospital ward 'seriously'?

11 Why do you think the writer, Brian Clark, shows Doctor
    Emerson battling to improve hospital resources? (See his
    telephone conversation about the monitoring unit.)

12 Outline Doctor Emerson's arguments in favour of
    administering Valium to Ken. What arguments are put
    forward by Doctor Scott in support of Ken's view?

13 Why has Ken decided that 'life isn't worth living'?
    (Look at his conversations with Mrs Boyle and Dr
    Scott.)

14 Why is Doctor Scott upset after her conversation with
    Ken? Why is Ken different in her eyes?

Act Two

1   What does Ken want Mr Hill to do?

2   During his conversation with Doctor Emerson Mr Hill
    says, 'I begin to see why (Ken Harrison) thought it
    necessary to be represented'. What does he mean?

3   How does Doctor Emerson explain Ken's desire to die?
    What is Mr Hill's response to this reason?

4   How is the Mental Health Act of 1959 going to help
    Doctor Emerson?

5   What is Doctor Emerson implying in his conversation
    with Doctor Scott? (Look at the speech beginning, 'I'm
    sure it's not necessary for me to say this but . . .')

6   According to Ken, how does a doctor treat his
    'customer' differently from a way a sculptor treats his
    customer?

7   Doctor Travers says that Ken's intelligence 'weakens' his
    case. How? (What does 'Catch 22' mean?)

8   Why did Ken send his fiancée away? Was he being
    'generous' in his view?

9   What do you learn about Ken's parents and their
    attitudes?

10 What is the difference between suicide and euthanasia? Which word best describes Ken's intentions?

11 Doctor Scott tells Ken that she thinks he does not want to 'win' his fight to die. What evidence does she use to support her argument?

12 What is 'Habeus Corpus'? How does this law apply to Ken?

13 Why does Ken find John 'a tonic'?

14 Ken says that the hospital is being deliberately cruel. How does he justify this statement?

15 Outline Ken's justification to the judge of his decision to be allowed to die.

16 Why does Ken refuse Doctor Scott's kiss?

17 Is the ending what you hoped for as you read the play?

2 Explorations

The following are suggestions for work of your own arising out of the situations and issues in the play.

1 Write the scene in which Ken tells his fiancée not to come and see him again. (Her name is not mentioned in the play, so invent one for her.)

2 Write a letter from Doctor Scott to Ken's parents in which she tells them what happened when the judge came to the hospital, and what will happen to Ken over the next few days.

3 Imagine that after the events of the play Nurse Sadler decides she does not want to be a nurse. John takes her out and tries to change her mind. Write this as a short story.

4 The judge's decision has been leaked to the press – write the newspaper article. Make it a front page item and include comments from as many of the people involved as possible. Include an 'Editor's Comment' section on the page in which the Editor says whether he agrees or disagrees with the judge's decision.

5   Write an obituary for Ken Harrison. (You should look at an obituary page in a 'quality' newspaper to get some idea of how this is done.)

6   Using a tape recorder or video camera put together a short documentary on the subject of Ken Harrison's death. Interview the main characters in the play in order to gather their views and feelings.

7   Is suicide wrong? Using the various arguments contained in the play use this question as a starting point for a group discussion. (This may be used as a GCSE oral exercise.)

8   Use one of the following titles for a short story of your own:

   a) The Accident

   b) The Hospital Visit

   c) The Patient

3 Essay questions

1   *Whose Life is it Anyway?* is about Ken Harrison's determination to decide his own fate, and about the determination of those who care for him to keep him alive. What are the arguments used by both sides?

2   How far do you think *Whose Life is it Anyway?* is a play about the individual versus authority and bureaucracy?

3   How does Brian Clark try to avoid sentimentality in his play? Do you think he succeeds?

4   *Whose Life is it Anyway?* was originally written for television (although the text here is the theatre version). What evidence is there that this was a TV play? Do you think it would be more effective on the stage or on television?

5 What view does *Whose Life is it Anyway?* give of the medical profession? Do you think it is a fair view?

6 Describe Ken Harrison. Do you think that Ken Harrison's personality and background helps or hinders the play's discussion of free will?

7 Write two letters – one from a parent expressing disapproval that this play should be studied in school, and a reply from a student defending the choice of the play for GCSE work.

8 How far should an individual have free will? Using the play as your starting point, discuss this issue in relation to Ken Harrison and, in broader terms, to issues in your own life.